"This book gives you a profc
that has the power to trc
Each chapter will enlighten your life
with new found wisdom and energy."

Lili Fournier
Producer, Director and Host
of the Award winning Quest series on PBS

POWER TO
BLOOM

By *NASSRINE REZA*

with a Foreword by John Selby

Power To Bloom

~~~~~~~~~~~~~~~~~~~~~~~~~~~~~~~~

~~~~~~~~~~~~~~~~~~~~~~~~~~~

FOREWORD

by John Selby ThD

author of *Quiet Your Mind*

~~~~~~~~~~~~~~~~~~~~~~~

I don't usually find myself reading inspirational books these days – they so often repeat the same old ideas from a slightly different angle. Therefore I was deeply pleased, when asked to review and edit Nassrine Reza's new book, to discover a pure gem. It's quite reminiscent of Krishnamurti and Hafiz, but delivers its own full-fledged punch of just-emerging wisdom and spiritual clarity.

Nassrine was brought up in Switzerland with her Iranian father and Russian mother. Such mixed influences probably opened insight-doors for her, revealing the universal human condition in a new and simultaneously ancient light. Her vision without question multi-cultural. However, having now come to know Nassrine quite well, I've found that her perspective on life transcends cultural influence – she's looking deep within her own heart to intuitively perceive truths that transcend culture and philosophy.

In this book Nassrine offers us a direct inner path to connect with the foundational life-knowledge within each of us. Her innovative voice will also impact the fields of mystic awakening, personal development and spiritual psychology.

Recognized at an early age to have the ability to instantly perceive a person's medical condition, Nassrine regularly works with patients and groups, sharing her insights into human nature and fulfillment. For the last decade she's traveled the world leading seminars, conferences and retreats. In 2002 she came forth with a new method for enhanced healing and wellbeing called Nutri-Emotion, focusing on the natural correlations and interactions of water, emotions and physical health. Collaborating with psychologists and doctors, in 2014 she published her first book (in her native tongue of French) called *Nutri-Emotion, A New Way of Healing and Self-Realization.* In 2016 she published her bestselling book *The Power of Acceptance – being reborn in a single instant,* which has been very successful in French-speaking countries.

Along with her writing, therapy, and seminar work, Nassrine is a gifted musician, currently composing and producing a new musical production. She's also an inspired creator of short video monologues which allow Spirit to communicate new insights and revelations. She's now creating an interactive website and app to accompany this book.

Power To Bloom is unlike any book you've read before. It quite succinctly examines a number of ingrained themes and beliefs that often hinder our lives. I've read each of these short insight-units many times now, and they keep revealing more and more hidden aspects of myself – that's their special evocative power.

I want to state clearly that this book is definitely not intended as a traditional intellectual/philosophical discourse. Nassrine has what I can only call the overt audacity to challenge dozens of our cherished notions about how to manage our minds and emotions.

Perhaps the first time you read some of these insight units, you'll find yourself curiously reacting to what she's saying. I urge you to temporarily let go of traditional assumptions, and contemplate deeply what she's suggesting. While reading these insight units from start to finish, you'll find that a spontaneous process of awakening is stimulated, helping you to unveil what you really are.

The book has been structured in seven parts. Each part explores a special perspective regarding the natural consciousness through which life fully blossoms. While reading these pages, your ingrained identification with who you think you are will begin to dissolve naturally, allowing you to experience your original state.

Power To Bloom isn't designed to change the world – instead, it sheds much-needed light on how we as individuals can accept what we really are, attain inner freedom, and enjoy the pure pleasure of being alive right now. With much enthusiasm and thankfulness I welcome you to Nassrine's realm of fresh perspective, stimulating insight, and revelation.

John Selby
Santa Cruz / November 2018

PART ONE

The Human Being

~~~~~~~~~~~~~~~~~~~~~

When you have the courage
to leave all your previous
knowledge behind you,
then you gain the power
to make your own discoveries.

GETTING RID OF ALL THEORIES
~~~~~~~~~~~~~~~~~~~~~~~~~

If you want to discover the truth
about what you really are
you first have to get rid of theories,
even the most attractive ones.

How many times must we prostrate ourselves before others? How many times must we believe that someone else knows better than we do, is more intelligent and worthier than we are? How many times have we listened passively to others, swallowing their various concepts about karma, mission in life, the idea of being a soul, the power of positive thinking, the latest wellbeing technique, and so forth?

Who really knows what's right and good for each of us, if not ourselves? Who, except ourselves, can possess our own interior truth, which is not a concept at all?

You might ask yourself the following: "Was I born with the concept that I am an emerging soul, with a specific mission in life? Was I born with the idea that I must analyze all the events of my life, and constantly struggle to become the best version of myself? Was I born with the assumption that I must somehow fulfill my true nature? Was I born with the belief that life consists of making mistakes so that I can learn from them?"

Did you ever hear a young child talking about such things? Did you ever see a young child dedicated to using positive thinking, the law of attraction, a healing method, or any form of visualization?

There are many theories about what you are, what you should do, and how you should behave. All of these theories enslave you. You see yourself only as a student, forgetting that you are your own master and guide. You constantly compare yourself to others, forgetting that you are a unique being, and that no one except yourself can serve as an example to you. Trapped into a huge mental web filled with countless concepts, have you lost sight of your own energy and wisdom?

You were born a free being – and you have the right to color and shape and determine your life with your own energy! If you would genuinely like to go back to your initial free state, I invite you to stop accumulating more theories, and avoid any comparison to others. This is where your new journey begins.

THE POWER OF ACCEPTANCE

~~~~~~~~~~~~~~~~~~~~

*The great paradox is that
our inner strength lies in
relaxing and accepting what is
rather than habitually
denying and fighting against
the reality that we live in.*

I remember my encounters with a beautiful four-year-old child called Lili, who was suffering from leukemia. For her birthday I gave her a Teddy bear, and she played joyfully with it like any other child would. Even in her hurtful situation, she wasn't consumed in thoughts such as "I have to be strong, I have to focus and fight against my disease" – children are naturally free from any such fixations on inner resistance.

It is in this state of ultimate acceptance that each human being is born. But then we grow up and forget this natural state. In the course of time and under the weight of social conditionings, our attitude towards life becomes transformed into a constant inner struggle against ourselves.

We habitually use a huge quantity of energy in order to mute the body's symptoms, forgetting that pain is a precious messenger. We try to eliminate all negative thoughts, and by doing so we reinforce them. Meanwhile our deepest feelings remain buried under the most common fear of humanity – the fear of not being loved.

All these mechanisms of resistance not only transform a human being into a robot, they also transform the experience of life into a battlefield. However, at every single moment we can make a choice: we can invest our energy in resisting all that manifests within us, or we can rediscover our initial state – unconditional acceptance.

By listening again to the 'earthly team' of our body, mind and emotional system without trying to constantly manage them, we can free ourselves to rediscover our natural equilibrium. And when we replace self control with inner acceptance, we naturally open the doors wide to embrace our own well-being – because well-being is fundamentally the absence of any form of inner struggle.

WELLBEING
~~~~~~~~~~~~~~~~~~

Wellbeing is quite simply the absence
of any form of inner struggle.
When we give up struggling
against life's expressions
our many problems
naturally disappear.

Humans are constantly in search of the wonderful and healthy feeling of wellbeing. But what can we do to achieve this inner contented state? Fundamentally, wellbeing is best defined as the absence of struggle. But wait – there is struggle everywhere, even when we're not always aware of it.

Observe yourself in your daily life. How often do you get caught up in conflict? The driver in front of you doesn't go fast enough; your partner doesn't understand you; your child has problems at school; your body still hurts. All these situations are synonymous with struggle.

Unfortunately, the interior act of struggling is what usually perpetuates the problem. Struggling against a problem doesn't really help to resolve it – and in fact, struggling inevitably makes it worse.

I was recently giving support to a lady suffering from cancer. Her husband, working in the military, continually asked her to be strong and to actively fight against the disease. He was unaware that his urgings were primarily intended to stifle his own fear.

At the appropriate time, I told him: "If you give your wife the right to be vulnerable, to embrace all of her feelings, you will allow her to find the strength necessary for her recovery. And please, do the same yourself – this graceful act of surrender and acceptance will significantly ease the agony for both of you."

In similar spirit, I invite you to be very attentive to any form of inner resistance occurring in your daily life. And when you notice that there is a struggle, don't try to get rid of it. Trying to break away and release something is fundamentally an act of resistance!

So – just observe that there is struggling. You'll soon also see that by staying aware but not interfering with the struggle, it will naturally fade away.

The less you do regarding struggle, the better you'll feel.

NURTURING

~~~~~~~~~~~~~~~~~~~~~

Three primary forces dwell within you:
your body, your mind, and your heart.
When you balance them equally
and nurture them all with kindness
they will become your best allies.

Anoki, a Native American boy, was carefully watching the village healer providing care to an ailing woman. Part of the healing ceremony involved blindfolding the woman. At the end of the treatment, Anoki asked the healer why he'd blindfolded the woman.

The wise man sat down and took Anoki on his lap. "You know, adults easily lose sight of what's important," he said quietly. "With the blindfold, she can see the essential. Being cut off from the outside world, she can perceive the messages of her three inner dimensions."

"What dimensions are you talking about?" Anoki asked him with curiosity. The healer explained: "Three forces dwell within you: your body, your heart, and your mind.

14

If you don't nurture each of them properly, if they lack attention and sustenance, they'll rebel and eventually you get sick. By getting to know all three dimensions that live within you, you can discover what they need and how to satisfy their hungers. To do this, you must learn to fix your attention on your body, mind, and heart without being distracted by the outside world. It is for this reason that I've blindfolded this woman."

But Anoki was still full of questions: "So what do these three dimensions like to eat?" he asked. The healer said quietly: "The body thrives mainly on water. The mind hungers for peace. And the heart thirsts for love."

Overall well-being is indeed based on these three pillars: water for the body, peace for the mind, and compassion towards negative emotions in the heart. When you're faced with any imbalance, I recommend this:

1) Drink plain water on a regular basis – do this with your eyes closed while breathing calmly.

2) Tell the mind it is free to openly examine and choose what is right and good for your overall wellbeing.

3) Welcome the negative emotions, and if you can do so, smile to them as a sign of compassion.

YOU ARE THE ONE
~~~~~~~~~~~~~~~~~~~~~~~~

If you wake up tomorrow morning
feel simply happy for being alive –
all the rest is secondary.

When you woke up this morning, what was your first thought? Did you think about your next holidays, about your bank account, about all the things you have to manage today? Or were you aware of the most important point – that you are alive?

While you were comfortably sleeping, thousands of people didn't survive this night. Perhaps you assume that being alive is something very normal – that opening your eyes to a new day is quite commonplace. But your life could end right now. I don't tell you this to induce a reaction of fear, it's just a fact. We never know when the body will take its last breath.

A participant told me one day, euphoric: "I'm looking forward to going into retirement in two years!"

"Well, perhaps you shouldn't be so delighted about this", I replied.

"But for my entire life I've been waiting for that moment. I'll then finally have time for myself, and I will enjoy life fully. Why shouldn't I be glad about my retirement?"

"For the simple reason that you don't have any guarantee to get there alive," I responded with a smile.

When we're really conscious that this moment could be our last, then we enjoy it fully and don't waste our energy with futilities. Our order of priorities naturally changes. And before going to bed, we accept that we don't know if there will be a tomorrow.

Perhaps there are things we haven't expressed to the people we love, because we thought we'd have many opportunities to do so in an illusory future. But – the only opportunity we have is called 'now'.

So don't waste another minute. Grab your phone if you'd like to share something with the people you love – go for it right now. And if tomorrow morning you open your eyes to greet a new day on planet earth, then you can smile for being alive.

EXPERIMENTING

~~~~~~~~~~~~~~~~~~~

How can you know
the taste of a fruit
if you just
look at it?

A participant who was attending my seminar, asked: "I've spent many years searching for the meaning of life – when will I finally discover it?"

I replied: "Tell me, how many years did you spend simply living life, rather than trying to discover its meaning? Perhaps a burning desire to comprehend the meaning of life drives you every day, but do you ever dare to fully dive into the pure experience of life itself? You have so many questions and that is perfectly fine. But ask yourself for a moment: what have you really come here seeking? Are you only looking for some grand theory or meaning – or do you long inside for a real change, for an encounter with living truth beyond all meaning?

You ask me what life is all about, and I answer you: A well-educated person observes and analyzes a piece of fruit and can write a long history about it. But he can never claim to know its flavor until he has actually tasted it and experienced it directly.

Looking for a great meaning to life can become a utopian endeavor in frustrating futility. Do you need to decipher the notes of a song in order to hear the music and let yourself be moved by the experience? You can spend your entire life creating great concepts – or you can leap in and discover the essence of life.

Always keep in mind that your life is like a piece of fruit that slowly, in a lifetime, withers away. Why are you waiting to live fully here and now?

If you could drop all your questions and your personal analysis, you would be living spontaneously and continually within the experience of life itself – and this experience would naturally offer you all the answers you need.

What choice do you make now?

COMPARISON

~~~~~~~~~~~~~~~~~~~~~

Since you are a unique being
you can never compare
yourself to somebody else.

Just take a moment and choose two of your own positive qualities, and also two of your flaws.

And now ask yourself: on what basis it is possible for you to define your qualities and flaws? The answer will probably be clear: only by comparing yourself to somebody else.

This is what we do most of time. For instance, we can only consider ourselves a generous person because we are comparing ourselves with somebody who is not. But fundamentally, such comparisons are a totally fictitious and fruitless process, because there are about seven billion people living on planet earth – and every single human is unique. Each individual has its own special feelings, its special thoughts, its specific shape and color, its individual memories, yearnings and wisdom.

Because of your uniqueness, comparison is an illusion. So are your qualities and flaws. One day I met a young man who was complaining about his hypersensitivity. He told me that he wanted to get rid of it, because his hypersensitivity prevented him of having a normal social life. "I just want to be normal!" he admitted, exhausted.

I responded: "You will never be normal, because you are a unique being. And because of your uniqueness, you can't compare yourself to somebody else. Normality doesn't exist! Your sensitivity is neither too much nor not enough. It is totally in tune with your own energy, and it serves you in your daily life. When you stop struggling against that sensitivity, when you totally accept it as a gift, then you can use it in a powerful fulfilling way."

If we stop comparing ourselves to others, then we can really enjoy what we are, and nurture the special gifts we have. Life is generous. Life gives us exactly what we need in order to discover and fully use our own unique talent and potential.

THE TRUE SOLUTION
~~~~~~~~~~~~~~~~~~~~~~~

There is no need to try
and find a solution.
Life spontaneously offers
solutions when we stop
searching for them.

I have some good news that will greatly simplify your life: you no longer need to struggle to identify problems and find solutions – because true solutions effortlessly arise when you stop searching and struggling, and instead allow your life to unfold naturally.

In the greater view of life, we in fact have no need to plot and plan and manipulate the world around us in order to live the good life. When we observe how people's lives develop, we begin to see that everything of importance happens spontaneously as a natural ongoing universal flow of feelings, insights, and events.

This is not a utopian notion that I'm talking about, it's the simple clairvoyant recognition that human beings are in their essence an integral part of life on this planet,

22

even if we are no longer aware of this integrating fact. The only flaw in us is that we believe ourselves to be separate from life. This inevitably leads us to struggle to manipulate everything in order to survive. With much effort, we continually strive to blossom – we take a unified harmonious whole and break it up into separate disjointed antagonistic parts – isn't this a crazy paradox?

If you allow yourself to experience each moment as flowing with life while it unfolds, instead of always trying to control it, then every problem will naturally turn into a solution.

How exactly can we learn to do this? It is very simple! Just step by step, begin to banish any vocabulary that induces the notion of effort. Choose to put aside and forget all programmed ideas such as "I must, I should/shouldn't, I have the will to, there is still work to do…" And here's the key – don't replace these expressions with anything else. Instead, stay quietly tuned into your breathing and your feelings and your spontaneous actions in this emerging moment.

This simple mental shift will give you a new perspective on life, as you discover for yourself that for every problem, there is always a solution!

AUTHENTICITY

~~~~~~~~~~~~~~~~~~~~~~

The best gift you can give others
is not your smile
nor your kindness,
but your authentic presence.

Do you remember the last time you felt completely free? For most people, such a memory goes back to their childhood, because often this was their only carefree period of life. Most young children have an incredible natural ability to be genuine in their feelings and act freely, spontaneously, without inhibition.

But in adulthood if not long before, this natural ability to be genuine gets seriously hampered by a fear-based need for social acceptance and external recognition. The original qualities of spontaneity and naturalness fade away and may even disappear completely.

I encourage you to pay attention to all the various social masks you wear on any given day. Notice that none of them manage to express who you really are behind the mask – masks by definition are hiding the real self.

I'm sure you would like to rekindle that feeling of lightness and freedom of expression that you once knew. What can you do to recreate honesty and spontaneity in your inner world? I invite you to proceed as follows:

1) Find opportunities to honestly say "no".

2) Avoid justifying or defending yourself.

3) Congratulate yourself often.

Acknowledge your uniqueness, bravery and freedom whenever you manage to be honest and genuine. You'll see how being authentic allows you, and everyone around you, to feel free once again.

Humans everywhere are taught how to be polite, kind, helpful, respectful, effective, smiling, loving, conformist. But almost no one teaches us how to be authentic, even though it's our authenticity that encourages honesty, sharing, communication and growth. So let's allow everyone to be who they really are at every moment – and this must start with our own inner feelings.

THE WORST THING IS CALLED HOPE
~~~~~~~~~~~~~~~~~~~

The worst thing you could have is called hope.
Hope represents the highest level of resistance
toward what you're experiencing
right here and now.

"I've made so many efforts in order to fix my dilemma, and now I deeply hope that everything will be fine," said a man who was experiencing a difficult situation.

"But perhaps hope is the main problem," I responded.

"I don't understand – I've always thought that hope is a positive constructive energy," he reacted, confused.

"I know this sounds illogical," I explained. "But people believe in lots of things that they haven't fully examined. Let's look deeply at the mental act of hope. It is actually a judgment and rejection of what we're experiencing in our present moment. When we hope for a situation to change and improve, we're actually saying 'no' to what is actually happening right now."

If we totally accept our current situation, we never even entertain the idea of hoping for something other than what is. In this light, hoping for change makes us believe that our current situation is some kind of error. Clinging to hope maintains the illusion that our situation should be different – but life doesn't make any mistakes.

The present moment by definition simply is! We're always at the right moment in the right place living exactly what we're here to live. But we'll never see the perfection of life itself, as long as we are holding hope in our imaginations about living a different future. I realize this is hard to grasp – but wishing things would be different cuts us off energetically from fully participating in the moment. This logic is important to embrace.

The man replied: "I've never considered hope in that way. I've hoped and I've prayed for so many things, but it's true – I was always caught up in a deep struggle while doing this."

When we let go of our hopes and prayers, when we abandon all our wishes, even the most beautiful ones, then we're able to recognize the perfection in every emerging moment of our lives.

SIMPLICITY
~~~~~~~~~~~~~~~~~~~

Life at its essence
is utterly direct and simple
if you can somehow manage to
simply stop making any effort
and allow life to unfold naturally.

Isn't it amusing to see how much you value making an effort and exerting willpower, while at the same time you're complaining that life is too complicated and your tasks overly burdensome? It's paradoxical but common for most humans to think: "I work so hard, it's no fun, but look – I'm succeeding!"

If you're honest with yourself, do you really like challenges? They make you feel important and promise wonderful outcomes – but most of the time, the challenges that you take on for good purposes tend to end up feeling like an obligation. You burden yourself with all sorts of challenges, you strive to accomplish them, and convince yourself that completing them will improve your life. But will they really?

Success isn't the issue. If you look as a neutral witness to see why you take on so many difficult challenges, you'll probably find that you're habitually craving recognition. You believe that being seen by others as struggling under duress will generate high rewards.

Yet, in a healthy life, what do you truly need? You need your own loving recognition, not the positive judgment of others. And you need to be recognized in your own pure presence as complete, whole, beautiful and fulfilled – even when doing nothing at all except ... being.

You can do this for yourself right now – simply choose to accept and honor and love yourself just as you are. In making this ultimate inner act, you will immediately enjoy the pure simplicity of life without challenge.

Nature offers a wonderful example of this. Its growth and endurance, beauty and value is based on a process free of judgment, effort, or willpower. This natural process is the same for humans. To maintain a healthy relationship with your body, mind and emotional system, I recommend that you congratulate them every day, especially when they do things with simplicity, fluidity and fun! You will then find that life becomes light and easy and exciting.

TRANSFORMATION
~~~~~~~~~~~~~~~~~~~~~

Transformation begins
the moment you stop attaching
any importance
to how you see yourself.

Keeping your self-image frozen in who you were or who you want to become is the greatest obstacle to inner transformation. Maintaining a self-image that's stuck in memory confines you within your limiting beliefs.

For instance, there's the belief that any profound change requires lots of time and effort. In truth, transformation can take place in no time at all, and with zero effort. This is accomplished by consistently rejecting any self-image that is generated by memory and repetition.

This approach may seem trivial, but it is much more powerful than you might imagine. Just hold in mind that you don't have to struggle to reach any goal —

because everything you desire and aspire to is already present at some level in your life at this very moment.

There is never a path leading to fulfillment, to healing, to awakening or personal development or unconditional love – because these are always right now omnipresent. You don't need to free yourself from anything, because nothing has the power to imprison you.

Take a look at your cherished or despised self-image and you'll realize that the person you think you are doesn't exist – it's merely the product of an assemblage of ideas in your memory. If you constantly work hard to change the ideas you have about yourself, nothing will be transformed.

Only sleeping beings believe that life consists of a series of intentions and mental repetitions. A free being perceives novelty at every moment and in everything. It doesn't approach life through memories and plans, but through a continuous openness towards discovery.

So you can just relax and take a fresh look at every situation, every gesture – and especially, behold anew the people you already know. See nothing as frozen. And so begins the transformation …

PART TWO

The Body, A Miracle

~~~~~~~~~~~~~~~~~~~~~~~~

"When you're totally conscious
that the body is a miracle
then you don't
underestimate it anymore."

LIFE IS NOT A STATISTIC

~~~~~~~~~~~~~~~~~~~~~~~~~~

Life isn't a statistic.
Life is a vast mystery
that can't be grasped by
averages and projections.

We tend to think that every aspect of life can be reduced to a statistic – but the beautiful thing about life is that its subtle underpinnings remain a mystery. There are over seven billion human beings right now – and they're all unique. How could we possibly reduce life into a statistic, while every physical body is continually expressing itself in its own special way?

I once knew a wonderful person known as 'the stone woman.' Since her childhood she ate little stones each day, because she was living in very poor conditions in India. Finally, after a long healthy life, she died at the age of 114. Because of her unique diet, her body was studied at several research institutes in Europe – and no illness nor lack of vitamins were found.

I don't invite you to eat little stones, but to open your mind to the idea that the body can survive quite well in very difficult conditions. My father-in-law for instance should have died at the age of two because of an intestine cancer. He's now 71 and has had 12 different cancers. His doctors still don't understand how his body has survived, literally living with cancer for 69 years.

The body is without question more powerful than we assume. The first living cell came into being billions of years ago. And the human body has evolved through the toughest times on earth. Its wisdom is as vast as the universe itself. The only thing that definitely erodes our body's health is the negative impact of chronic stress. I've known many people with very healthy lifestyles, who died quite young – and all of them were suffering from chronic self-inflicted emotional stress.

I invite you to put aside all your concepts and concerns about what a healthy life could be – and instead consciously support your body, your mind and your emotional system when they're facing stress. Drink plain water on a regular basis, and relax the body as often as possible. Remember that your unique physical miracle developed itself during nine months without cognitive help and worries. You can definitely trust it.

THE OBVIOUS FACT

~~~~~~~~~~~~~~~~~~~~~~~~~

*Understanding is not necessary
because acceptance is quite
sufficient unto itself.*

One of my patients was suffering from an autoimmune disease. She had already moved through several different analytical therapies, and she explained to me: "Thanks to lots of introspective work, I finally discovered that I was actually afraid to get well. I have realized that because I'm sick, my relatives take care of me. But if I heal, I'll no longer be their focus of attention – and I'm quite honestly scared to be left alone. I just don't know what I can do in this predicament. I'm stuck."

"You have found a plausible logical explanation," I responded, "for how it is blocking your own healing – but do you think this revelation will trigger healing? You've undertaken a number of therapies and they have helped you view your illness from an intellectual standpoint. It's common for people to cling to such explanations – but in reality, your body hardly needs your intellectual explanations in order to heal."

My patient looked at me, puzzled, and added: "But if I can't use my thinking mind to stimulate healing, then what on earth can I do?" I took her hand gently and placed it over her heart. "Your body basically needs you to accept it just as it is right now."

Tears ran down her face as emotions flowed. She relaxed and hugged herself with her arms. I said to her, "Your body doesn't understand intellectual interpretations – but it can feel if you are with it or against it. Instead of staying in denial, you're now free to embrace reality and allow your body to be sick – and to heal."

She nodded. When I saw her later on, she was healed.

So let's stop hunting for reasons and feeding our minds with explanations. Doing so negatively blocks our ability to fully accept our body's current situation. And only when we accept our inner reality, can that reality begin to loosen up and change, heal, and recover its natural balanced healthy state.

INTERPRETATIONS
~~~~~~~~~~~~~~~~~~~~~

*If we need to know something
specific about the body's condition,
our intuition will spontaneously
bring it to mind.*

After hearing me talk about the futility of searching for a conceptual causal model related to illness, a participant in my group exclaimed: "But what you're saying is in total opposition to all I've heard till now!"

"Well, that's quite possible, but tell me what is bothering you?" I asked in return.

"I believe that every single pain and problem in my body is a messenger. For example, liver problems are all related to anger issues."

"Did your own liver tell you that?"

"No, of course not, I found this information in a reliable book written by a well-known medical authority who explains his theory in clear scientific detail."

"But life isn't a theory," I suggested. "Perhaps you should let go of theories, and instead talk about your own body's actual experience."

I then explained my understanding that, even if an author insists emphatically that a liver problem stems from an anger issue, the body doesn't understand such convoluted logic. And in order to heal and remain healthy, the body doesn't need intellectual guesses and lofty explanations.

Every body has its own frequency, its own way of functioning, its inherent wisdom. It's impossible to establish a universal law or statistic for seven billion unique organisms. What each body needs is the absence of struggle, of inner resistance. If the mind is relaxed, the body will relax – and then it can get on with its natural healing work, quite serenely.

The body is much wiser than what we can imagine. Birds and deer and worms and dolphins don't need to develop complex intellectual constructs in order to stay healthy – they accept life as it flows, and this acceptance isn't correlated to any form of analysis. If we need to know something specific about the body's condition, our intuition will spontaneously bring it to mind. Life is indeed at heart, that simple.

NATURE
~~~~~~~~~~~~~~~~~~~~~

Spurred on by our splendid inventions
we are constantly searching for new solutions,
forgetting that Mother Nature our earthly cradle
already offers us everything for free.

A medical scientist heard of a Hindu doctor with a clinic in the hinterlands, who was giving very special medical care to his patients. Intrigued, the scientist decided to go and meet him. After trekking through a vast tropical forest, he arrived in the middle of a big field. A single large house was standing there. He approached and entered and was introduced to the famous doctor.

"This healing center doesn't look at all like our modern hospitals," the scientist noted with amazement. "Your patients sleep on bunk beds and living conditions here are quite primitive."

"If the beds for my patients were too cozy," the doctor told him with a smile, "they would never want to get out of them. How could they possibly heal this way?"

40

The scientist laughed, thinking it was a joke. But he was further baffled when he saw some patients, barefoot, out pulling weeds in the garden, and even plowing the fields. Others were sitting under a tree, some were singing and others meditating in silence. He could not conceal his astonishment: "So that's your method of healing? No hospitalization or medication?"

"The best hospital is nature itself," the doctor responded. "Nature provides all the medicinal plants my patients may need. We do not consider disease as a curse, but as an inner call to reconnect with the source of all life, which is none other than Mother Nature."

Stunned by these words, the scientist asked: "And people heal through this approach?" The doctor looked at him and replied: "The body was fashioned by the forces of nature. Put it back in its original environment and you will see positive results."

The scientist then spent two years with the doctor, exploring the remarkable benefits of natural medicine, where the best way to restore health is to live in the primordial embrace of Mother Nature, who provides for all our needs, free of charge.

PURE PLEASURE
~~~~~~~~~~~~~~~~~~~~~~~~~~

All of life is a playground
but as adults we no longer
give ourselves permission to play.
Set your inner child free again
and your whole life will blossom
with renewed health and satisfaction.

Pleasure is a powerful tool that helps increase and balance the energy flows of the body, mind, and emotional system. Notice that, when left on their own, children play most of the time. They know instinctively that joy is highly beneficial to their immune system and stimulates the body's natural growth.

But as children are sent to school and then become adults, this natural human lightheartedness tends to be replaced by a more rigid and reduced energy that step by step impairs your three allies of body-mind-emotion.

Ask yourself: "For how many minutes or hours yesterday did I have genuine fun?" For most adults, this answer can be stated in seconds or in the best case, in a few minutes. In comparison, list all the things that upset or stressed you yesterday, and how many hours you spent consumed in the opposite of fun and joy. Did you push yourself to work without a break?

If you're like most people in our society, you know that there's a major flaw in how you chronically neglect to surrender to pleasure. We're a workaholic culture that denies pleasure. We all suffer greatly and without mercy because we accept the prevailing 'all work – no play' attitude toward how we spend each new day.

Do you understand now that your days are more like a battlefield than a playground? And as you listen to the inner needs of your body, mind, and emotional system, are you ready to actively enhance your day with fun? What's preventing you right now from shifting into pure-play mode? Nothing at all!

So what are you waiting for? It's definitely time to set the wild child within you free to play again! Good health and recurrent moments of pleasure are inextricably linked. So cultivate pleasure, take time each day for fun and you'll definitely increase your overall sense of vitality, creativity and joy.

THE BODY, A MIRACLE
~~~~~~~~~~~~~~~~~~~~~~

*When you become conscious
that the body is a miracle
then you won't continually
underestimate it anymore.*

Right at this moment, your body is performing millions of functions simultaneously. Are you aware of this? In this very moment, millions of cells are dying. Does that worry you? Ever since your body was conceived, your heart has been beating non-stop. Do you have to make any effort to keep it working?

This wonderful physical miracle of the human body is so sophisticated that no human hands could ever replicate it. And in its vast complexity, it skillfully and effortlessly manages itself – mostly without any effort or conscious guidance on our part. Just provide some plain water and a bit of food on a regular basis, provide exercise and shelter and companionship, and there you have it! Isn't that amazing? Isn't that miraculous?

Usually we become quite concerned about our body's functioning only when it manifests a negative symptom. Otherwise we trust our own organism to perform its constant miracles without conscious attention.

The first living cell came into being a very, very long time ago. Since then, the cell has adapted to a vast number of changes and constantly evolved, giving rise to a highly-sophisticated human body. Today perhaps more than ever, life is being confronted with unexpected non-organic disruptions – because the water, air and food that living cells require are more and more polluted. But, believe it or not – the body can adapt!

On the other hand, there is a factor which the body will never get used to: psychological stress. Mental stress is not something normal – it indicates that our inner endurance has reached its breaking point.

We urgently need to take time often each day to ease up, breathe consciously, regain our inner composure and give loving space to any emotion welling up. This is the best natural path to preserve and recharge the energy resources of our body, mind and emotional system.

PART THREE

The Mind

~~~~~~~~~~~~~~~~~~~~~~~

"If you think that your mind
is an agitated being,
it's only because you didn't yet
discover its true nature."

CONFIDENCE

~~~~~~~~~~~~~~~~~~~~~~

Gaining more confidence is
a goal so many people aim toward –
but what is confidence?
It is just another mostly-meaningless word.

There are always people who come to me in order to somehow develop their confidence. They believe that if only they can gain more confidence, they'll become powerful and live a more successful life. I often ask them: "What does confidence mean to you?" They usually can't answer this question in a meaningful way. Perhaps lofty psychological descriptions emerge, but behind all the words and concepts and beliefs there seems to be – nothing of practical human worth.

Can you define confidence? Is it a specific way of thinking or a particular attitude that you can somehow make an effort to acquire or adopt? So often we latch onto and chase after mostly-meaningless goals.

Confidence is just a concept, among so many other concepts that we've been conditioned to aspire toward gaining, in order to feel better and succeed at higher levels. But is there really anything behind such words?

Perpetuating these supposedly life-saving ideas and ego-boosting goals generates lots of money – because many programs and courses are offered to people who rush in, hoping to find and possess some invisible quality or power. People who have not yet questioned their beliefs and goals can be easily manipulated.

I suggest the opposite: choose to stop being trapped by words. Stop trying to attain some presumably-missing quality or skill. When you were a child ready to climb on your bicycle the first time, did you ask yourself if you had enough confidence to do this experience? No. Confidence is not something that you can buy or attain. Fundamentally, confidence is your mind's natural state.

What if you don't need to strive to attain anything at all in order to feel fulfilled and satisfied? Why not just relax and enjoy this moment, and naturally discover that everything you've been looking for can already be found right here right now, deep within you?

SEEING INSTEAD OF BELIEVING
~~~~~~~~~~~~~~~~~~~~~~~~~~~

We create our own prison
when we are perceiving everything
happening around us
through the chronic projection
of imagined expectations
generated by ingrained beliefs.

A young man was out walking in nature and found himself suddenly face to face with a big spider on its web. The young man panicked, jumped with fright and screamed for help. The village elder, who was busy gardening, approached him. "What puts you in such a state?" he asked.

Paralyzed with fear, the young man pointed his finger at the creature and whispered: "I'm afraid of spiders, they terrify me. Last year, I was bitten!"

With a smile on his lips, the wise man said, "Right now you are not seeing the spider, only the fear that you project onto it. In this moment, you only perceive your old memories."

The young man felt anger rising in him and curtly retorted: "Old man, you have such poor eyesight that you can no longer see clearly!" The learned man gently came closer and whispered: "Your mental projections permanently impair your eyesight. See what is there and not the idea that you have about it. Then your fears and your memories will vanish, and you will be able to live peacefully."

The wise man went away and the young man, who remained overwhelmed by all his fearful emotions, didn't notice that the spider had now comfortably settled on his shoe, causing no harm at all.

All our beliefs stem from a single place: our past experiences and memories. When we choose to turn away from the past, and perceive the present moment with fresh fearless eyes, we find that our fearful reactions are almost always outdated illusions that we continue to project onto the new moment. This is always our choice, and herein lies true freedom and peace.

DON'T BE TOO SERIOUS
~~~~~~~~~~~~~~~~~~~~~~

*How can you live a
life filled with lightness
when you take yourself
so very seriously?*

A man joined my seminar on the theme "Don't be too serious!" At first, he listened intently. Then after several minutes he spoke up and said to me: "Excuse me, I didn't understand everything you were saying."

"It doesn't matter," I responded. "Life doesn't need to be understood, we simply have to live it."

Surprised, the man asked, "But what can I do if I didn't understand anything?" "Well, I responded, smiling to him, "Instead of understanding everything, I invite you to stand up and dance in front of everyone."

"Are you kidding me?" he reacted. "I'm not a clown!"

"The crux of this problem," I reflected, "is that we are constantly caught in a process of self-identification, which makes us control what we do and think – so rather than dancing and enjoying this moment, our thoughts keep us bogged down in overwhelming heaviness. Life itself isn't serious at all."

Touched by these words, he did – he got up and began to dance around like a carefree clown. A deep joy emanated from him, and laughter filled the whole room. After a few minutes, he exclaimed, euphoric: "I didn't know that I loved dancing that much!"

Every day, we need to encourage ourselves to be less serious. Every day, let's give ourselves the right to stop judging ourselves, so that we are free to clown around, to dance and sing and laugh and hug spontaneously.

I encourage you to invite yourself quite often each day to do things you never dared to do, act out with frivolous behavior that doesn't really matter. In this way you will learn to approach your life with more lightness – and this quality of lightness flowing through in your mind, body, and emotions will inevitably help untangle all your problems.

BEING PROUD
~~~~~~~~~~~~~~~~~~~~~

Humility is a very attractive concept
but it has nothing to do with
the human's initial inner state.

Humility is a common concept in many spiritual approaches. But if we observe life, rather than following theories about how to behave in our lives, we discover that humility has nothing to do with life itself.

When we observe a young child, we find out that there is no humility present at all. In fact, a healthy happy child is often feeling very proud. This pride has nothing to do with arrogance, it's just a natural positive energy that the child experiences and uses in a very constructive way. What do I mean by this? To explain, let's do a simple exercise:

For the next few moments, bring to mind several things that you have bravely done, and done well, so far in your life. And also observe how remembering these well-done actions makes you feel right now. Do you notice that your energy is naturally increasing?

54

Most young children have plenty of energy. This has nothing to do with their age – it's instead directly related to that particular feeling of being proud. This is a feeling that energizes and nurtures all the cells of the body, and also enhances the energy of the mind and emotional system.

But as we grew up, we tend to lose that special connection with our own self-esteem. We come to believe that we can only value ourselves if we do quite exceptional things. And even if we accomplish them, we are often not really satisfied. Why? Because we think that we're still not good enough.

When we fail to regularly hold ourselves in high esteem, then we get stuck desperately waiting for somebody else to do it. But even if the whole world was feeling proud of us, this adulation wouldn't nurture our inner space, because our inner space requires our own recognition.

So – I encourage you to be generous with yourself and feel proud of your everyday accomplishments, even feel proud when you don't do anything – be proud of who you are now! This is the best way to enhance your energy and create a beautiful relation to your "earthly team' of the body, mind and emotional system.

LET LIFE CARRY YOU
~~~~~~~~~~~~~~~~~~~~~~~

There's no need to trust life —
because life constantly supports you anyway
without any effort or precondition.

Imagine you're lost and all alone, floating in the middle of the ocean with no land in sight. There are two possibilities for you – either you start swimming in a random direction and probably die of exhaustion, or you let yourself relax and drift wherever the waves and currents naturally carry you.

There are natural waves and currents in life itself. They effortlessly carry to life's shore those who choose to surrender their direction to them. Sometimes the water is calm, sometimes it is stirred. But those who have become fully aware of their state of oneness with life itself no longer attempt to swim against the tide. They come to understand that they are part of a perfectly established equilibrium, and they can surrender themselves to this overall equilibrium with complete peace of mind.

Seen another way, it's not the individual flower that chooses to open and bloom in the sunlight. It's the sunlight's power, it's the energy of life that enables and encourages the flower to open. And it is the same for us humans. We don't really decide out of the blue to get up in the morning. It's the life-force flowing through us that stimulates us to get up and participate in the new day.

This wake-up response is a spontaneous movement that constantly occurs at so many levels in each day of our lives. But it seems that most of us are no longer aware of this – we mistakenly believe that life must be controlled and dominated, thus provoking a futile struggle against life, and against ourselves.

If you have grown weary of this resistance to life's flow that constantly depletes your inner space, you can do the following exercise every night before going to sleep:

Just lie on your back and spread your arms and legs. Breathe effortlessly from your belly and relax and say to yourself several times, "Whatever the waves may be, I consciously choose to let myself be carried along by life."

SELFISHNESS

~~~~~~~~~~~~~~~~~~~

Don't feel guilty for being self-centered
and taking care of your own needs.
If you're not living for yourself first
then what is the point of living?

Selfishness is often seen as a bad trait that must be fought and abolished – but at the same time, selfishness plays an essential role in your life. Most of what you do each day is designed to take care of your own needs and desires.

Even when you're helping others, you do this partly because these acts of kindness fill you with joy. There's inescapable evidence that all human deeds are ultimately motivated by our selfishness. And regularly satisfying our personal needs and focusing attention on our own wellbeing is a natural survival mechanism inherent to all of life.

Perhaps in your life you have often been criticized for being selfish – but should you feel guilty because you are being fully attentive to your inner space? If none of us took responsibility for satisfying our own needs and desires, our entire civilization would collapse.

Besides, consider what drives others to aim guilt at you for taking responsibility for your own wellbeing. Do they want you to take responsibility for their wellbeing at the expense of your wellbeing? Perhaps it's only your profound inner freedom that bothers them.

As a basic mature rule, it is our legitimate right to live our life the way we want to. What is unfairly selfish is the habit of expecting others to live their lives according to our wishes and beliefs. If we want to set ourselves free, it's essential that we also grant that freedom to all others.

In the spirit of being authentic, I recommend that you never feel obliged to spend your time with anyone, or to accept a request that does not resonate deep down inside you.

This freedom of choice and action is the finest thing you can do for yourself and also for others.

TRANSPARENCY

~~~~~~~~~~~~~~~~~~~~~~~~

*Honestly saying no
can be the best help ever
for yourself and for others.*

How many times have you said 'yes' to a request from a friend or stranger, when in your gut and even your heart you actually want to say 'no'? Do you think it's socially impossible to reply with, "I'm not willing to help you now?" Would that be so awful? Why does it seem so terrifying to be honest and transparent?

How long must we still play this universal game of polite dishonesty, whom does this game of artificial support actually benefit in the end? Neither you nor the other benefits through failing to be honest with each other. After all, if you don't live your life for yourself above all, then why live?

Perhaps it's time to finally begin listening to our inner space, give ourselves this precious gift! Let's all dare to openly decline the requests of others if our inner self doesn't resonate with doing the request.

Please realize and remember that you are not responsible for the situation or experience of others. You can remove this burden from your shoulders. Everyone lives their own experiences, and all experiences are beneficial. So you are free to eliminate any guilt feelings when you say 'no' – and furthermore you can praise yourself when you honestly admit what you think and feel.

There is nothing negative about not being willing to help others when helping doesn't feel right, but it is bad both for you and the others to pretend otherwise. Let yourself recognize that you are doing the best you can, and that you and the others are already perfect.

By paying attention to the honest messages arising from your inner space, you will allow others to do the same. When you are unable to help people, you allow them to use their own internal resources.

Isn't this a very good thing?

DISAPPOINTMENT

~~~~~~~~~~~~~~~~~~~

By giving up all your expectations
you can avoid feeling disappointed
ever again.

Did you ever think: "I have so often been helpful to my friends, but when I really need them, they're usually not willing to help me?"

This rote expectation of future help or payment or recognition for something we offer sets us up for getting hit with disappointment and calling into question the value of our relationships. However, this disillusionment isn't really caused by actions or inactions of others – it's rooted in our own inner expectations that are often unfulfilled. We unconsciously project our hopes and needs and desires onto others, and when their behavior fails to correspond to the expectation we're anticipating, disappointment inevitably follows.

It's very helpful to take time to reflect on just how pervasive our expectations are – in fact, most of our actions stem from them. Like a thirsty animal, we expect the outside world to quench our desires.

When we help someone without expecting anything in return, or when we complete a task in a heartfelt manner that demands no response, we will live our lives free from disappointment. When we understand that results and reciprocations don't matter, because the essential joy lies in what is being experienced now – then we're truly free to enjoy the moment.

With this in mind, we no longer need to frame a relationship through our own requirements. And rather than focusing our attention on the always-uncertain future, we relax and enjoy what we're doing right now.

To help you let go of all forms of expectation, I recommend that you use the following sentence when you find yourself expecting something from the outside world: "Dear expectation, dearest wish, I thank you for being here and trying to satisfy my needs, but please know that everything in my life is already perfect right here, right now."

By accepting the moment and giving up expectations, you'll notice that life almost magically begins to offer you much more than you imagined.

EDUCATION

~~~~~~~~~~~~~~~~~~~~~

We must grant everyone the freedom
to choose what they want to learn
based on both their passion and their talent.

The mother of a three-year-old child told me about her wishes: "I want my son to be a great violin virtuoso, he has all the abilities and opportunities to succeed. I never had the opportunity to do what I wanted, so I want to give him all the education he needs." I looked over to the child, who firmly held his violin, and invited him to leave the room for a few moments. "Does your child like playing the violin?" I asked his mom.

"Oh, if only you knew how well he plays already!" she replied proudly. "You did not answer my question," I told her. "Well," she said, suddenly hesitant, "a three-year-old child cannot yet know what he likes. His parents must show him the way to success, the way to professional performance."

"I won't pretend to tell you how to educate your child," I said, "just make sure you don't transpose onto him

64

your own expectations and shortcomings. Your father didn't allow you to become a violinist, right?"

Her face suddenly changed and showed a deep sadness. She sighed: "Indeed, I had all the potential to carry out a solo career, but my father believed that studying academic courses was more important. You know, I just want my child to be happy."

"If that is true, I suggest you tell your son he can freely choose his passions. In doing so, he will discover what really drives him, and you will thus create a fulfilling relationship with him."

"But he's too young to decide anything for himself," she complained. "Perhaps even at three," I suggested, "he has the ability to express what he likes, how he wants to spend his time – it's all a matter of you learning to listen without trying to influence him."

"But it's the role of the parent to influence the child," she insisted. "Oh," I responded, "I thought it was the role of the parent to help the child step by step grow into discovering and expressing who he naturally is."

THE DEMANDS

~~~~~~~~~~~~~~~~~~~~

When you are determined
to transform your life
the transformation process freezes —
so stop urgently insisting.
This is how change begins.

"I'm tired of all your complaints!" said the husband in an exasperated tone during a counseling session. "Me too, I've had it up to here with you!" objected his furious wife. She turned to me: "I told you, it's impossible to talk to him. He never understands me. Maybe we should split up, this conflict has lasted so long."

"Perhaps talking isn't the problem," I replied in a neutral tone. "You'd both be much happier if you stop investing your energy in trying to change each other. Of course, you are free to split up, but that wouldn't change the underlying problem – you'd probably soon find yourself with a new partner who forces you to confront the same difficulty. Your partner is not the obstacle to the solution."

So what is the obstacle?" the woman demanded. "The obstacle," I replied, "is how you perceive and react to your own emotions. Your partner, as well as anyone you hang out with in life, is reflecting emotions that you've so long rejected."

"Well then, what should I do?" she insisted. "You would do much better in life," I recommended, "if instead of being at war with your feelings, you welcome them with open arms. Give them space within you to resolve their tensions – only then will your relationship disputes ease up and cease."

When you are dealing with an angry person, or someone who's anxious or overwhelmed by sadness, you might tell them: "You have both the right and the need to contact that emotion, and I invite you to welcome it as it is right now."

The emotional conflict will dissipate, not because you're expecting a change, but because you finally allow all the emotions to be present.

MADNESS OF POWER

~~~~~~~~~~~~~~~~~~~~

*If we take seriously what
is said in praise about us,
we will have big problems
to manage.*

The daughter of a president in a rather violent country desperately contacted me one evening. Her father was in an alarming situation, threatened with violence by some malicious people. Anguished, she asked me, "I beg you, tell me what my father must do!" I took a few breaths and then replied: "What needs to be done will be done." Still frightened, she continued, "But what should be his strategy to avoid any danger?" I looked to my inner voice and then repeated: "There is nothing to do."

Here's what she passed on to her father: "Nassrine said to do nothing, so just relax and don't go out of your hotel room at all tonight." The next day she called me, euphoric: "You have an amazing gift! My father was supposed to go speak at the place where a bomb exploded last night. Thanks to you, he didn't leave his hotel room – how can we ever thank you?" Surprised, I replied: "I never told him to stay locked up, I simply said that what was to happen would happen. You are the one who gave the specific suggestions to your father. Thank yourself for this."

But she failed to understand my words and proceeded to talk about the event and present me as the "supreme seer of the year" – I had to stop answering her calls, and strongly discouraged her from attributing to me any kind of illusory power.

Likewise, I recommend that you never allow anyone to put you on a pedestal. If you take seriously what is said in praise about you, you'll have a big problem to manage! Imagine being told that you are the most insightful person in the world, and that you always find a solution to everything. That's way too much pressure! You would have to try and live up to that reputation that's been imposed upon you.

Put the authentic power of others back into their own hands, and quietly manage your own without fanfare. If we all do this, much of the chronic madness of power will cease in this world.

THE TRUE NATURE OF THE MIND

~~~~~~~~~~~~~~~~~~~~~~~~~~

The more you observe your mind
the more you will learn
about its true nature.

Many spiritual, psychological or personal-development writings are constantly telling us that the mind is fundamentally an agitated mechanism, and it must be controlled. In order to manage it, we're invited to use various tools such as meditation, visualization, positive thinking and so forth. But if you've already tried these mind-management techniques, you've realized that your mind is still functioning in the same manner.

If we pause and discover the mind for what it really is, instead of what we've heard about it, we come to realize its inherent intelligence and sensitivity. A baby, for instance, doesn't have any thoughts at all. It is moved and informed directly by the life force itself. Its mind is a quiet empty space, free from anticipation, questioning, theory and analysis – and yet the baby still functions.

But over time, the mind gets filled up with more and more ideas, imaginations, concepts, information and disinformation. Educational, social, environmental and religious conditioning store in the mind a vast collection of concepts and assumptions that make the basic intuitive function of the mind struggle for space.

Imagine that your mind is like the room in which you're sitting. Your mind is the space in the room, not all the furniture. There's no need to blame the room if there are too many pieces of bulky furniture. Your mind simply houses the information which has been stored inside its space – all the thousands of anxieties and prejudices and beliefs and strategies acquired from your parents and your social and religious education.

Fundamentally your mind has a powerful primary function – receiving and acting on information from your intuition. But unfortunately there isn't enough free space in your mind for new intuitive information.

I suggest that you collaborate with your mind. When worried or manipulative thoughts and beliefs dominate your inner space, remember that you once functioned quite well without being ruled by attitudes and projections. Your mind was born free from conceptual domination – and you can regain that freedom!

PART FOUR

The Conditioning

~~~~~~~~~~~~~~~~~~~~~

"Any form of struggling
stems from the conditioning."

CONDITIONING
~~~~~~~~~~~~~~~~~~~~

When a man has a millstone
around his neck since birth
he easily forgets its presence.

All human beings accumulate a heavy mental backpack filled with information, attitudes and disinformation they never chose to take on. This baggage – the cognitive and emotional programming that the brain receives especially in early childhood, is our social conditioning.

This conditioning step by step comes to dominate and literally take over personal expression and behavior. And it generates an exhausting inner struggle between our core intuition and direct response to a situation, and our conditioned reaction that's often in direct contradiction to our instinctive response.

However, such a constant inner struggle isn't part of our true nature. Like a defective gene, this mental struggle has been imparted into our mind's activity by fear-based programming. And, each time we resist,

74

ignore, or distort a pain, a thought or emotion, the mental conditioning gets even bigger. In fact, most of our personal actions are a result of this conditioning - but we too easily forget its presence.

How many times have you found yourself in a situation where you're reacting in a particular way that you don't understand, despite much introspective work? How many times have you vowed to permanently change some of your behaviors – only to quickly backslide into negative programmed patterns?

Because most of your problems are caused by this conditioning from the outside world, those problems actually don't belong to you. And when faced with a situation generating internal resistance, I recommend that you keep this phrase in mind: "This situation is not of my making, but nevertheless I accept it."

When speaking, notice who is actually using your mouth. Is it your inner wisdom, or your conditioning? If your communications express doubt, analysis, anticipation, judgment or any form of struggling, the conditioning is talking. By observing consciously and without resistance what is going on in your mind, body and emotions, you can realize and banish the influence the conditioning has on your body, mind and emotions.

YOUR INNER STRENGTH
~~~~~~~~~~~~~~~~~~~~~~~~~~

Your inner strength is not
the result of an act of will.
Your inner strength lies in your
ability to live with your own energy.

If you'd like, choose a present difficulty in your life: a pain, a conflict, a fearful thought, an upsetting emotion or some particular situation. Observe this difficulty for a few moments without doing anything, just breathe freely and accept its presence.

And now ask yourself: "To whom does this difficulty belong?" You'll usually find that the perceived difficulty is being generated by inherited or adapted attitudes and beliefs. Your belief system has been implanted in your mind mostly by your parents at an early age – it's not natural organic human nature.

As you begin to realize that your conflict-generating, fear-based beliefs and reactions have little to do with your true nature, it becomes easier to accept each situation without wasting energy feeding belief systems.

76

In a natural free life, nothing is done against you, but always for you. The life force continually encourages you to free yourself from all inherited beliefs. And when you regain this freedom, you're able to discover and feel proud of your own unique energy and wisdom.

Watch a very young child. It never thinks about struggling to ignore or eliminate the present moment. It welcomes every single emotion without analyzing or trying to overcome it. Why? Because it doesn't yet have a belief system that judges each new situation in life.

Who's telling you that your responses of sadness, fear or anger aren't acceptable emotions? Who's telling you these emotions have to be controlled or released? It's always your conditioning that does this – that parental authoritarian voice in your head that every day pushes you to struggle against and try to control and alter your natural body, your thoughts and your emotions.

Conditioning is based on trying to avoid fearful situations through self-management and control. We run away from everything we fear, including fear itself! The wise move is instead to openly welcome and embrace fear and other so-called negative emotions when they arise. Make room in your heart for all your emotions – and you truly become free and whole.

LOOKING FOR SIGNS
~~~~~~~~~~~~~~~~~~~~~~~~

*The conditioned mind is continuously
looking for meaningful signs and omens.
We are taught that the universe is trying
to signal us with subtle meaning.
But does nature really play these
symbolic omen games with us?*

Does a black cat, or the number thirteen, or a fluttering butterfly or the color violet evoke some special meaning or significance for you? Many people consider an entire array of naturally-occurring images and happenings to be important universal symbols that we learn about in books, folklore and family tradition.

What happens when your conditioning reads and believes that sighting a fluttering butterfly is a harbinger of a profound transformation coming your way? This insect will suddenly be incredibly important to you and when you see one near you, you'll be convinced that life is sending you an important message. Driven by this belief, you will scan the horizon, eagerly waiting for a profound change to come your way.

Do you believe that life keeps placing signs in your field of vision, so that you detect a message essential to your evolution? Do you think that life, God, whatever you call it, likes playing such subtle riddle games with you?

If human evolution had to wait until every human being finally tunes into the presence of subtle signs indicating what to do in life, humanity would still be in its infancy. Looking for signs in nature, projecting significance onto everyday occurrences, this is only a game that the conditioning plays with itself, not a grand scheme of subtle communication that the life force is playing for our personal benefit.

Life is not a riddle, life is a natural force we're all flowing within. And this life force does not throw symbolic challenges to humans, insisting that we interpret natural phenomenon as alleged symbols to influence our lives.

At every moment, the life force is guiding all human beings so that they may be in the right place at the right time. No more and no less. There's no need to decipher life. It's sufficient to simply live and enjoy it now.

LOVING FREELY

~~~~~~~~~~~~~~~~~~~~

Real love is a love without any reason.
It lives in the heart, not the head.

The love we are going to talk about here isn't a conditioned love that demands anything of the other person — it's a deep spontaneous feeling that involves no coercion, no compromise, no sacrifice. We all are born with this capacity to love. And when our natural human quality of unconditional love prevails, we are free of all expectations, and cannot be disappointed.

Let's take a common example. Let's say you enter into a relationship with another person, and come to believe that you require this person in your life in order to feel useful, valued, happy and fulfilled. You've been conditioned with an underlying false belief about what true love is. In contrast, the reality of true love is that no other person is responsible for helping you attain a genuine sense of fulfillment in your heart.

Perhaps one day your partner rejects you and leaves you. You suddenly fall apart emotionally and feel abandoned and lost – and you blame the other person for having disappointed and hurt you. Believing this person would complete you, you now experience abject loss – you feel that you're nothing without her or him.

The truth is, it's not the other who disappoints you, and furthermore it's not your authentic self who falls apart – it's an illusory self maintained in your conditionings, beliefs and thought system. And only when you come to truly love yourself unconditionally, without any reason, will you then be able to love the other simply for who he or she really is: a free being just like you.

When you come to love, accept, honor and enjoy your own true self unconditionally just as you are, you can enjoy every shared moment with another person, free from the fear of being rejected or left alone. You won't have to make compromises or sacrifices because everything is being offered spontaneously, and resonates with your own freedom to be.

When this inner clarity arises, you'll realize that the other is not present in your life to fulfill your needs or compensate for your illusory shortcomings, but to make you aware that you already have within you all you need.

CONTROL
~~~~~~~~~~~~~~~~~~~~

Life cannot be controlled,
the overall flow of life lies
beyond your manipulation –
but you can definitely learn to
navigate in harmony with the flow.

If you could for an instant experience freedom from all conditioned fear-based concepts, you'd see your true nature and never again try to control anything. The conditioned part of your brain has been filled with the insidious idea that a fulfilling life is attained through your controlling everything happening inside and around you. But the body is managing itself wonderfully well without any control of your manipulative thoughts – because your body already knows what it needs.

Negative thoughts naturally disappear when your mind's conditioning no longer strives to be positive. The emotional system also naturally frees itself from its blockages when there's no longer any underlying struggle. And harmony with other people emerges when you stop trying to control them, even supposedly for their own good. Without your interference, they will naturally discover what's beneficial to them.

Understand that any form of control reflects a deep fear of living. When you realize this, you will naturally stop feeding this control mechanism. The truth is that the infinite breadth of life cannot be managed. Even if you try extremely hard to do so, there will always be elements that remain beyond your control.

When you let go of struggling to control everything, you effortlessly gain the power to accept the flow of your life, and navigate serenely within that flow. As you regain a strong connection with your inner voice, you can successfully face all the vagaries of life. An unshakeable sense of wellbeing is never dependent on external circumstances – wellbeing emerges as a natural consequence of being continually plugged into your inner guidance system.

Imagine that you're floating effortlessly down the stream of life who's natural course can't be controlled. You don't know where life is taking you, so all you can do is surrender and adapt to each movement that life's flow brings you ... with ongoing joy and contentment.

QUESTIONS & ANSWERS
~~~~~~~~~~~~~~~~~~~~~~

We're taught that asking questions
is the best way to get answers.
And by doing so we forget an obvious fact:
The question always stems from the response.

Over the course of a single day, a large number of questions spring forth and jostle together in the heads of every human being. We're taught to continuously create questions and then to chase after the answers – but in fact, acting in this seemingly-logical way will keep the answers out beyond our grasp.

It has been agreed upon that logically, a question leads to an answer. Upon closer observation however, this is a logical aberration. The answer must always come before the question. At some level we must already know the answer – otherwise how could we formulate the question? One cannot exist without the other.

Life is ultimately simple. It can willingly give us all our answers before we even have time to intellectualize a question. Our challenge isn't to ask clever questions

and seek brilliant answers to our intellectual queries –
our challenge is to continually live fully in this emerging
moment where the true answer is obvious and appears
in our awareness at just the right time. To seek an
answer through asking a conceptual question is to make
a huge detour to get at the answer.

Rather than habitually seeing your life as a series of
problems and questions to answer and solve, what if
you accept your life just as it is, observe where it is
naturally flowing – and surrender fully to that flow?
This is always the challenge: to stop worrying about
your life, and just relax and live more spontaneously.

When the next question pops into your head, I invite
you to observe that question dispassionately – and then
choose to let go of it.

Feel free to tune into your breathing and your
experience in this emerging moment, and focus your
mind on the following sentence:

"The answer to my question is already here, arising
naturally into my awareness at the right moment."

PERCEPTION
~~~~~~~~~~~~~~~~~

How we perceive the world
depends on the labels
we attach to our perceptions.
When we choose to take away the labels
we can see the world clearly.

The people and situations we perceive all around us are like a large painting upon which countless labels and judgments have been superimposed, getting in the way of our actually seeing the picture before us.

Often, we see the labels, judgments and assumptions of our own conditioning more distinctly than we see the reality in front of us. Whenever we eat food, chat with our neighbor, or listen to a song, it's almost impossible to break free from all our projections and associations so that we can experience and relate with present-moment honesty and integrity.

I invite you to try the following exercise. Choose any food and ask yourself if it tastes good. Then ask yourself the question, "What defines whether this food tastes good or not?" Do you think your taste buds give you this information? No, they can only determine if the food is somewhat sweet, salty, sour, bitter, hot or cold.

So then, who gives the verdict of the food tasting good or bad to you? The conditioning, of course, which is invariably half-blinded by its various beliefs about the food. The food has neither a good nor a bad taste. It's just food, it's just energy.

Likewise, the next time you talk to a friend, observe all the judgments that your conditioning may have about her or him. When you are aware of all those projections upon your friend, then these labels will instantly fade away. Look at your friend and just remember that she or he is a perfect human being, like you. This new dynamic will reinforce the relation to yourself and to others.

Also, choose a song that your conditioning doesn't like. Listen to it carefully. What appears as dissonance or bad taste doesn't arise from the song itself, but from the interpretation and judgment of the conditioning.

If you observe the functioning of your conditioning then you will realize that behind all the labels hides an absolute neutrality.

YOUR PARTNER
~~~~~~~~~~~~~~~~~~~~~~

If we don't project any conditioned picture
onto our life partners,
we set them free to
more fully emerge into
who they are continually becoming.

Maybe you have already experienced a situation in which you suddenly felt you could no longer even recognize your partner because she or he has somehow changed. Your partner does or says something unusual or different from before, and you feel like you're facing a stranger. Why such a turnaround? What is happening in such a moment of confusion and misunderstanding?

The conditioning resembles a vast library in which every person, idea, and expectation is carefully filed in its specific folder. What's in your "partner" folder? In general, we find defining words such as love, kindness, understanding, safety, listening, romanticism, tenderness, sexuality, desire and esteem.

Your partner probably corresponds to at least eighty percent of these descriptions. But then there comes a

88

jolting moment when your partner seems to have changed, perhaps seems to have lost the sense of romanticism. Before, she or he regularly prepared candlelit dinners for the two of you. Why did your partner stop doing this?

Your conditioning perhaps panics because one of the criteria no longer coincides with its "partner" folder. Fear manifests itself and doubts arise. "Does he or she still loves me?"

But the most important question is not "Why has my partner changed?" but "Why do I try to confine my partner in a particular image?"

Your true nature, beyond all the clinging fears of abandonment, aspires to express unconditional love – a love without ties or beliefs or requirements of any kind.

Only the conditioning is projecting predetermined requirements on the other. When you realize this, you're able to see your partner with fresh, accepting eyes. You will understand that true love is limited by none of the words in your "partner" folder – and you'll also set your relationship free to evolve in unexpected spontaneous directions that nurture both of you.

THE CORPSE
~~~~~~~~~~~~~~~~~~~~

The past is like a corpse
that continues to stink
in the present moment.

"In your teaching, you say that we have to leave all our past behind in order to feel fulfilled in the moment," objected one participant, "but there are not only bad times in my past, there's all the good times as well."

"I don't invite you to let go of your past because there are bad times in it," I replied, "but rather because all of those times are dead and gone, both the good times and bad – so it's helpful to stop dragging this corpse of the past around with us."

Another participant added: "But we can learn from our past." And I answered: "Did you ever see a dead body talking to you? When you think about the past, you literally exhume that corpse from its memory tomb and desperately try to resuscitate it in order to get some information which could be helpful to your present situation. Seeking answers from the past doesn't change your present moment. The past, that corpse, stinks with decay in the present moment, it carries dead and distorted memories which are usually useless. Why? Because every single moment is a radical new experience – but we cannot see the newness of it when we're dragging the corpse of the past around with us."

"I'm a therapist," said a man in the room with an angry voice, "and I invite people to refer to their past so that they can free themselves from their actual suffering."

"Suffering itself stems from past memories projected onto the present moment," I responded. "Why should we make a detour into the past to arrive at inner peace which exists only in the now? It's important to look and acknowledge that all forms of suffering exist only in the memory corpse and never inside our present moment."

I invite you to verify this right now. Close your eyes and focus your attention to this present moment. Do you now see any form of suffering? Is there any kind of problem in your present moment, when you don't add any thoughts and memories to it?

PART FIVE

The Emotional System

~~~~~~~~~~~~~~~~~~~~~~~~~~~~

"We keep our emotions imprisoned
as long as we try to
manage them."

VIOLENCE

~~~~~~~~~~~~~~~~~~~~

*Violence is the last outcome
of our inhibited emotions.*

"I killed three people," said the young man sitting with me in the room. "I'm a murderer!" he continued with a threatening voice. "I lived in Sarajevo and three men from a gang came to my house one night. They killed my wife and my one-year-old son and laughed at me while I was crying. After that, the only thing I wanted was to revenge my wife and my son. I waited three years to approach them, then at the appropriate time I killed them – and I thought the agony would disappear. But my suffering didn't leave me with their death. I'm no better person then those bastards."

"What did you want to kill when you were on the way to kill those three men?" I asked.

"Just leave me alone!" he answered aggressively. And when I repeated my question, he growled: "I'm going to kill you too, if you don't leave me alone!"

His eyes were filled with hate and suffering. I put my hand on his shoulder and said, "You've suffered enough. Give yourself the chance to be at peace. Your emotions still aren't free to express themselves, and so they create pain within you."

"It is because of these emotions that I killed the murderers of my family!" he exclaimed.

"Because your emotions were inhibited for too long, they finally had to act. You didn't want to kill anybody. You only wanted to eradicate that deep sadness. But it won't dissipate until you accept the sadness."

Suddenly, the young man stood up threateningly, lost in past memories. "You have endured enough suffering," I said to him. "Now you can choose to give yourself the chance to be finally at peace."

He stared at me. "I'm so sorry," he whispered, and as I held him, he was crying all his tears out from his body, releasing his inhibited tensions. I whispered: "You are now holding that old sadness in your heart. That emotion needs your help, it needs acceptance and unconditional love. This is how healing starts. You can be so proud of yourself right now!"

TRANSCENDING
~~~~~~~~~~~~~~~~~~~~~~~~~

When we invite an upsetting emotion
caused by a past painful situation
to rise up, be felt and accepted,
we experience inner peace.

I invite you today to carry out an experiment that will shape your life in a new way. Set aside five to ten minutes, and begin by standing up and letting yourself remember a past or present painful/upsetting situation. Notice that the moment this memory is reactivated, an emotion emerges and is felt in your body.

Now, notice if it's an emotion of fear, anger or sadness. Also, assess its intensity on a scale from zero to ten (ten being an unbearable emotional state). And then in one sentence, describe the painful situation to yourself and how it makes you feel. For example: "Two years ago, I lost my friend – and this makes me sad."

Now begin to imagine that this emotion stands before you. Observe it carefully for a moment – and then modify your sentence. For instance, no longer say, "two years ago, I lost my friend – and this makes me sad." Instead, say to yourself, "I observe that two years ago, a human being lost a friend – and that makes him/her sad."

While saying your own new sentence three times to yourself, at the same time bend your torso forward so that your head and arms dangle above the ground. And then, while you dangle, say three times: "I authorize this human being to merge with this emotion – and to be at peace with it now."

And now, lie on the ground and allow your body to relax completely, then begin to visualize the emotion warmly surrounding your body. Breathing calmly, stay in this position until the emotion has completely merged with your body.

Thank your inner space and yourself for this experience. Now, think back to the situation you selected at the beginning, and re-evaluate the intensity of the emotion.

You will find that the painful feeling has subsided, because you've transcended all its related resistances.

UNITY IS STRENGTH
~~~~~~~~~~~~~~~~~~~~~~

I had a dream. The dream to be myself.
Fear then gripped me tightly
in its arms and told me,
"If you dare to do that, your whole life will change.
I held fear by the hand and replied,
"Together, we will succeed."

During a consultation, I met with a father and his anxiety-ridden ten-year-old son. Early in the discussion, the father turned to his frightened fidgeting child and scolded him, saying: "Stop being so nervous, there's no need to be afraid! Come on, cut it out – there's nothing to be afraid of."

His son instantly contracted, he curled himself up in the chair as the anxiety attack ensued. The father seemed to have no awareness that his angry words and rejection were making his child feel terror-stricken. By trying to reassure him, the father was failing to give the child permission to feel afraid. Instead, he was unwittingly encouraging his son to try to fight against this natural emotion, which inevitably reinforced it.

And so, step by step the father learned how to communicate and be supportive in a new way. By recognizing and dealing with his own emotional repression related to fear, the father could then help the child break free from his anxiety attacks. The father no longer told him "Fear not!", but rather "You have the right to be afraid – and if you want, we can welcome your fear as a friend."

If you decide to allow fear to exist, you will find that you no longer fear losing others, and that you can dare to open your heart. You'll begin to trust your body and stop trying to manipulate its natural responses.

Fear is not a weakness. Ride with your fear, honor the feeling – and it may become your best ally. When you stop fighting fear, you can use that emotional energy as a force of utmost power.

So would you like to now hold out your hand to fear?

VISUALIZATION

~~~~~~~~~~~~~~~~~~~~~~

*Visualization seems to be
quite an interesting tool,
but in reality it actually
reinforces inner struggling.*

A lady who was suffering from breast cancer asked me very seriously: "I've heard about different techniques we can use to trigger healing. Do you think visualization could be helpful to my body?"

"The important question," I responded, "is not whether visualization might help, but why you want to use that tool. What emotion is provoking your question?"

She starred at me silently, looked inward, and after a moment she replied: "Actually, I'm really afraid. And so I hope visualization will help me heal."

"Visualizing health is actually a process of rejection," I explained, "because the intent of the positive focus is an avoidance of the underlying emotion associated with your condition – fear. By imagining a healthy body, you're trying to escape and resist fear – but through visualization you're actually reinforcing it."

I went on to explain that an emotion like fear is a very subtle energy, and when blocked and rejected, it must use a specific situation, like a disease, to get our attention. Rather than doing a visualization to get rid of a symptom, we first need to recognize the emotion hiding behind our current situation. Then we need to allow that emotion (in this case fear) to simply exist within us, along with all our other emotions.

By changing our behavior related to fear, it becomes free to do what it has to do. Fear isn't an enemy, it's incredible power to enhance our physical functions – but only if we don't reject it. The emotional system, the body, and the mind are like a family. If we're struggling against an emotion, the whole family will suffer.

When you choose to abandon your healing tools," I told the woman, "you create a space of unconditional acceptance. And within that open space, your intuition knows exactly what to do, every single moment in life – without any tools. So accept all of your emotions – don't interfere with that innate intelligence that dwells inside your body, mind and emotional system."

PRESSURE

~~~~~~~~~~~~~~~~~~~~

Feeling pressured to perform
makes us afraid to act.
Feeling loved and accepted
encourages us to
take the leap.

"Stop being such a sissy, David!" the father shouted at his five-year-old son who was learning to ski. "Come down the slope, we're not going to spend the whole day waiting for you – what's wrong with you, stop being so afraid."

Hurt by these words, David began to cry – and the father kept pushing. "Oh no, don't start that! Get down here or I'm coming up for you!"

I was watching the scene from a terrace and could not stop myself from skiing down and joining the child. "Hi David. My name is Nassrine. Are you OK?" The child snuggled in my arms.

The father skied up and joined us immediately. "Who are you?" he asked me curtly. "I am a ski instructor," I invented spontaneously. "Well you came at the right moment! My son is afraid to go down this ridiculous little slope. Perhaps you'll manage to persuade him."

I bent down and whispered these few words to the child: "You have the right to be afraid, David, but fear does not prevent you from having fun." His face suddenly brightened, he smiled, got up his courage, and went on down the slope.

Surprised, the father asked me, "What did you tell him? This is really unbelievable – the boy never obeys me."

"This has nothing to do with obedience," I told him. "Your son was not afraid of skiing. He was paralyzed because he was afraid of disappointing you."

When we accept ourselves and the emotions we're currently experiencing, we take away the pressure to perform – and in so doing, we gain access to our inherent courage to go out into life freely.

DEPRESSION AS HEALER
~~~~~~~~~~~~~~~~~~~~~~

Depression is a salutary energy
because it brings to light all
the buried and denied feelings
that have remained in the
dark for far too long.

"I feel so totally depressed, everything is collapsing around me, I don't know what to do, life seems so hopeless," stammered my new patient, who'd been suffering from depression for many years.

"Please consider," I offered, "that you are not depressed. You are instead witnessing a depression. And you can be proud of yourself."

"But proud of what?" she protested. "I feel devastated, dead inside, there's nothing but pain in my heart."

What is this condition we call depression that plagues a quarter of our population? It's best seen as a signal from our inner self telling us that all the blocked-emotion pressure accumulated in our past is over-ready to be released. And contrary to what most people think, feeling depressed can prove to be highly beneficial when approached without judgments – because the condition carries the potential to force us to break down, surrender and finally allow into the healing light of day all those early pent-up and denied emotions that have festered way too long in our guts and hearts.

We need to be courageous and choose to finally accept and express long-denied feelings that we've habitually blocked from open expression. We need to realize that we are witnessing this depression, and that it is not our deeper identity at all.

Look back and remember just how much and how long you've been struggling to control your own natural emotions. Thanks to the pressure of depression, those feelings can now have a chance to finally emerge.

My new patient learned to let go and break down and release all the long-buried anger and tears of her body. After a while she confessed: "Yes, I had pushed down and denied my real self for so many years, trying to keep control over my feelings. What a relief to allow them to exist."

~~~~~~~~~~~~~~~~~~~~~~~~~~~~~~~~

BEYOND ILL-BEING

~~~~~~~~~~~~~~~~~~~~~~~~~

*It is not life
that overwhelms you
and makes you suffer —
it is your conditioned reactions
and limited perceptions
that breed misery.*

Many, perhaps most people have been conditioned to think that life is the source of their suffering. "Life is hard and merciless," people often think. But from a more objective perspective, the flow of life is never directed against us personally.

Life maintains its fine balance of neutrality — but we cannot perceive this balance and neutrality as long as our attention is grounded in and directed by erroneous beliefs stemming from the conditioning. It is not life that overwhelms us and knocks us down, instead it's our behavior towards the events that happen that makes life beautiful or miserable. "Life is disappointing and unfair" has no basis in reality – this judgment is only based on the conditioning's interpretation.

Imagine the following example: you have organized a nice outing in nature on a mostly-sunny day, but the moment you walk out the door, rain begins to fall. Is the weather causing your upset feelings, or is it your reaction to the weather?

You can of course feel disappointed or angry, there's nothing wrong with that – on the contrary, by accepting your emotions you'll be able to refocus on your deeper feelings of inner peace. Allowing the free expression of your emotions enables you to approach all situations with lightness.

You are free to change your attitude toward the flow of events in your life. You can choose to stop feeling as if you are personally being targeted by difficult events. Such misunderstandings naturally dissipate when you are filled with a single intent – to see what is, and not what your conditioning projects onto life.

When facing any troubling situation, I recommend that you accept what this moment is bringing you, without trying to analyze it, but rather by simply opening your arms to all your emotions.

DON'T BEG FOR LOVE
~~~~~~~~~~~~~~~~~~~~~~

When we stop striving
to make people love us
we are free to love
unconditionally.

We've been made to believe that we absolutely need to be loved by others, in order to love ourselves. We're told to "be nice, polite, helpful, presentable, confident, and talented – then the world will love us." That's the universal human brainwashing that we have been chronically subjected to.

Unfortunately, we have been convinced that love has to be earned and deserved. What a sad life path, believing that we must make so many compromises, sacrifices and constraints, just to get a crumb of love. In our thoughts, beliefs and actions, we become beggars for love.

If you manage to recognize that there's never any need to beg for love, you finally become able to love freely. This means loving without any needs, expectations, or rancor. The role of others is in fact not to satisfy your needs and desires – and equally, you don't need others to satisfy your own heart's needs.

Believing that you do need others in this way can literally ruin your life. Such beliefs induce a form of dependency where the love you need to give yourself becomes fixated on trying to get that love from another person.

There are two forces that govern this world. One is called "love" and the other "the fear of not being loved". The first force enables you to act freely and with compassion in the world, not expecting love in return. The second force locks you into believing that you have to do various things in order to gain love, and in order to love yourself. Which life path do you choose?

You are fully capable of giving yourself all the unconditional love you yearn for, in vast abundance, all the time. This act of self-nurturing will eliminate any form of emotional subjection to others and you will become free again to love unconditionally.

MISSION IMPOSSIBLE

~~~~~~~~~~~~~~~~~~~

When you deeply understand yourself
you don't need to ask others
for mutual understanding.

We've often heard that it is necessary to put oneself in the shoes of the other person, so that mutual understanding can occur. Love is very often related to this idea. We assume that by understanding the other person, we can have a deeper and more harmonious relationship. But is it really possible for us to see life through the eyes of another person, even if they have experienced a similar situation to ours?

We would only have the ability of mutual understanding if we all were the same. But actually that isn't the case at all. Each person on earth is endowed with their own energy and inner experience, which is always highly individual.

During a consultation I met a couple who had been facing a relational problem for many years. Suddenly, in the middle of our discussion, the wife looked at her husband and shouted at him in anger: "If you really love me, you would understand my situation!"

I spoke up: "But your husband can't put himself into your shoes – because you're already inside them. There is no place for two people inside your shoes. You believe that he doesn't want to understand you, but in reality he simply cannot. You're asking for the impossible."

"But I thought that true love always included mutual understanding," objected the wife. "I don't feel loved when my husband can't understand my perspective."

"But even if you live together for many years, the two of you remain totally different people. Because of your uniqueness, you'll never truly understand each other. You must accept the fear inside you of never being understood by another person. When you are no longer afraid of being misunderstood, you won't ask him to put himself into your shoes."

We do need to honestly open up and recognize the fear, and all our other emotions – and allow that fear to exist within us. By doing so, we will come to more fully understand ourselves – and we can stop asking the impossible of others.

THE OUTSIDE WORLD
~~~~~~~~~~~~~~~~~~~~~~~~~~~~

The external reality that you
experience with your senses
doesn't exist in itself —
reality as we know it
is an internal creation
that we project outward
onto the world.

During one of my seminars, I asked participants to pay attention to some distinct aspect of their body, mind and emotional system, while listening to classical music. A state of well-being naturally flowed from this. Then we did the same exercise with heavy metal music. In less than ten seconds, most participants complained that these notes were unbearable to hear.

But what is a note? A note is a simple sound, a wave that carries energy. Nothing can be more neutral than that. But as the conditioning interprets particular sounds, it responds with emotional reactions and related thoughts.

I asked my seminar group three questions:

1) What emotion did you feel while listening to heavy metal? Most participants replied they felt anger.

2) Was it the music that created this anger, or your emotional system? In a short discussion, they all agreed that the feeling of anger came from within, not from without.

3) What happened when you felt angry? They all agreed that the conditioning aimed its angry emotion outward against the music. But was there a battle against the notes of the music? No, the conditioning wasn't attacking the notes, which are a highly neutral form of energy. It got caught up in fighting the anger itself.

When my group decided to experiment with accepting the reaction of anger, they were able to listen to heavy metal music while remaining calm and relaxed.

It's never the outer situation that generates a problem, but our reaction to the situation. And most of our reactions stem from the conditioning. It easily transforms life into a battlefield, if we don't observe it consciously.

COMPLAINING

~~~~~~~~~~~~~~~~~~~~~~~

Complaining is a natural messenger
expressing the need for change.
When we stifle the complaining
we block the discovery of
what's really bothering us.

We are usually brought up to believe that complaining is fundamentally negative – and that we should feel guilty when we complain. But when we block this natural emotional outburst of anger and dissatisfaction, we will never hear the wisdom behind the complaining.

Complaining is a powerful messenger, it's a legitimate and liberating act. It shows us that there exists a bothersome disharmony. Saying that we are fed up, that life is wearing us out, that we're in a bad mood – this expression is not negative in itself.

What's harmful is to refrain from complaining. People will say, "Yes, what you say is true, but things could be a lot worse – so don't complain." Does this observation that things could be worse help you? On the contrary, not complaining prevents the expression of blocked emotions that might help solve the problem.

Complaining is primarily the result of an anger that could not be freely expressed in the past. So open the door to this angry complaining and ask it: "Dear emotion, what puts you in this state?" Listen to it carefully. Let the anger speak, and that same anger, once expressed, will serve its purpose and then dissipate naturally.

I know this runs contrary to what most people think, but upon careful observation, complaining is an important signal from your emotional system that needs to express itself and be acted upon. It's a natural and highly beneficial mechanism for our overall well-being.

FEAR IS NOT A PROBLEM
~~~~~~~~~~~~~~~~~~~~~

I dare to follow my intuition
instead of listening to reason.

I dare to say freely what I think
rather than fearing the reaction of others.

I dare to make my dreams come true
rather than clinging to an illusory security.

I simply dare to live!

A lady who was suffering from anxiety attacks for several years, suddenly interrupted my seminar and yelled: "I can't handle my anxiety anymore! It makes me suffer every day, please help me!"

I invited the lady to close her eyes for a moment and bend her knees, and imagine that she was surfing a wave called "anxiety". While doing these little movements, I then asked her: "Is it the wave that makes you feel uncomfortable, or is it your reaction towards it?" The lady answered: "It's my reaction. I always try to control it, because I'm afraid of anxiety."

I continued: "Life is like a big ocean and you're in the middle of it. Can you control the waves? No. The only choice you have is to go along with the wave – or to swim against it. All waves are perfect, even if some of them are waves of anxiety, or sadness, or pain. Life knows that you're capable of welcoming this anxiety. Just bend your knees and with amusement, flow with that wave, experience it fully – and let yourself be surprised by what might happen when you stop trying to control life."

I saw the lady slowly start to smile. She was amazed – she said she didn't feel the grip of anxiety anymore. Her long-lasting problem had been resolved, without doing any analysis or therapy. So – what happened to her? Fundamentally she gave up all the resistance, gave up the illusory idea that she could somehow control life.

When we go along with all the emotions that life presents us, then we don't feel overwhelmed anymore. We can relax, stay in our center and enjoy every single second, whatever the wave may bring us.

WHO OWNS OUR EMOTIONS

~~~~~~~~~~~~~~~~~~~~~~~

We all share the same problems,
that's why personal problems
don't exist.

A young lady told me: "I've always felt very sad in my life and I really don't know why. I went through a lot of therapies, but they didn't help me. I don't know what to do with my emotion."

"Why do you believe that this emotion is yours?" I asked her. She looked at me confused and replied: "Whose emotion could that possibly be, if it's not mine? I don't understand what you mean."

I questioned her: "For a moment, remember your mother's life. Wasn't she sad very often?" She explained to us that her mother was dealing with a long-lasting depression during her lifetime.

I invited the young lady to ask herself the following question: "Did that sadness exist before you were born?" When she nodded, I asked her: "So why do you think that this emotion is yours?"

She looked at me puzzled. "But even if it's not mine, what can I do to free myself from it?"

"Obviously you can't free yourself from a problem that isn't yours. The problem is not the emotion, the problem is the belief that this sadness somehow belongs to you, and that you have to find a solution. The only thing you can do is to recognize that emotion and to accept it as it is. There's nothing wrong with sadness, even if it doesn't belong to you."

I invite you to pause and observe that all human emotions existed in human hearts before we were born. So how can we pretend being the owner of one specific emotion?

The problems each of us are facing are, in their essence, the same problems that our parents experienced during their lifetime. So next time, when an emotion appears, tell it this: "Dear emotion, you're not mine, but I accept you as you are."

ANXIETY ISN'T REAL

~~~~~~~~~~~~~~~~~~~~~~~~~

All our emotions stem from the past,
which is dead or from an imaginary future.
In the present moment, there is
no space for any emotion.

A psychologist who was attending one of my workshops explained: "Anxiety is a very important emotion, because it indicates to us if there is a danger."

I replied: "In fact, anxiety is a powerful emotion, but it's always related to the past, or to an imaginary future. If you were suddenly attacked by a tiger, you wouldn't have time to think of your danger and feel anxious – at that moment you would instantly respond physically to save your life. Only then, if you managed to escape, would anxious thoughts and emotions appear."

I went on to explain that anxiety always occurs subsequent to the present-moment stimulus. It's not a perception, it's a reaction to the perception, or an imagination about danger in the future – it's clearly a conditioned reaction. If our attention is fully focused

120

on the present moment, which is the only reality we're living in, then it is impossible to be anxious.

The problem is that we've been told that fear has to be understood and analyzed, if we're to free ourselves from it. But our search for a hypothetical cause is actually what generates anxiety and stress. The body doesn't understand the past nor the future. It only lives in the present moment. Trying to find hypothetical reasons for our suffering just makes things worse.

When we think about our traumatic past or a fearful imagined future, the body immediately reacts as if the experience is real in the present moment. Our breathing changes instantly and the body contracts, preparing to fight or run away. This causes stress, and stress intensifies anxiety. Stress is the worst enemy for our body.

At every single moment, our body, our mind and our emotional system receive thousands of sensory inputs related to the inner and outer environment. How can we find just one particular cause for our situation? Also, our memory is not a loyal friend – it creates a subjective story of our past. Life is so simple, if we focus on what is happening in our true reality – the present moment.

PART SIX

The Free Being

~~~~~~~~~~~~~~~~~~~~~

"There is no guide existing
outside of yourself."

BELIEVING YOU'RE A PERSON
~~~~~~~~~~~~~~~~~~~~~~

A human body was born and
suddenly you identified yourself
with that particular shape.
And from then on you forgot
your true nature.

Identifying fully with the physical body can be seen as the root of all forms of suffering. This identification keeps you caught in the illusion that you are nothing more than a physical body locked tightly in the space-time continuum of the manifest world.

Every morning when you wake up, your conditioning whispers to you: "You're an individual mortal person, you have a unique physical form with a name, memories and attitudes – and don't forget that you are seriously flawed and must struggle constantly to attain wellbeing."

A baby is born into a family, into a particular community and language and society. Surrounded constantly by these physical boundaries, that individual

124

develops a very limited personal and social identity. Continuous repetition of these limitations builds up a restricted image, so that the person grows up believing it is what it has been programmed to believe it is.

When I was a child, my parents gave me a beautiful bird. He sang every time he saw his fellow creatures outside on the edge of the window. With my heart torn apart, somewhat naively I decided to set him free. Much to my surprise, he never chose to escape. My parents explained to me that he didn't dare leave his cage, because he was born there. This prison had become his only home.

Your belief regarding who you are is a golden cage that gives you the impression of being limited at all levels, doomed to suffer and struggle and die. But your essence is in truth timeless and boundless – who you are cannot be reduced to a mishmash of cultural beliefs and assumptions and convictions.

Perhaps it's time to wake up from your dream. You don't need to break the cage or to find a way out – you simply need to realize that your prison only exists as a concept within your waking dream state. Your true nature is never limited to this manifest world.

THE LAW OF ATTRACTION
~~~~~~~~~~~~~~~~~~~~~~

We blind ourselves
with our own beliefs
about the laws of the universe.
When we put aside all beliefs
we become naturally reborn
into what life really is.

A therapist once proudly told me, "Thanks to the law of attraction, my life has been rebalanced in many respects. The law of attraction is a universal law because everyone has the power to attract what they want," she asserted. In response I said, "I humbly invite you to explain this law to an abandoned child who is dying of hunger."

Her enthusiasm suddenly dissipated. "Well – another law also applies, the law of karma – this child chose its life before incarnating" she replied hesitantly, her mind continually seeking a logical explanation for life, in this case through switching from the law of attraction to the law of karma.

126

But what do we actually know about all the laws of life that we've been taught to believe? If we talk about and believe in laws that we have learned by hearsay, we will never discover for ourselves anything really true about life.

What would remain if we would erase right now any conceptual picture we have about who we are and what life is all about? For instance, speaking of karma, none of us really knows where or who we were nine months before the birth of our body.

To discover our own truth, which is well beyond the law of attraction or that of karma, we need to explore openly and without any preconceptions what and who we fundamentally are.

As we enter into this exploration of life beyond concepts, we are able to effortlessly transcend all the boundaries and laws of this world, and encounter life without any concepts at all.

YOU ARE NOT AN EMOTION

~~~~~~~~~~~~~~~~~~~~~~

We often identify with emotions –
and by doing so we forget
that we're in truth
only their witness.

How many times have you told yourself: "I'm sad, I'm angry" or "I'm afraid"? Probably way too often! And by repeating those sentences, you finally identify yourself with those emotions. But who is really experiencing an emotion? None other than the emotional system, which is not in essence your higher identity.

Imagine that you feel anxiety, such as the fear of being judged, misunderstood, hurt or rejected. Now pause and quietly observe that fear. And notice that while observing the emotion, you're already separate and standing outside of it. How does this happen? Because you are not this fear, you are simply its witness.

In fact, it's impossible for you to be afraid. The following sentence, that you probably use a lot, is the proof of it: "I am afraid."

Realize that the "I" is your consciousness that observes a fear. Your true nature can never be afraid, it can only observe what's happening in the emotional system. When you stay aware of the various emotions, then you know as the witness that no emotion has the power to overwhelm who you really are.

So the next time an emotion appears, remember that you're its witness, not its prisoner. Remember to say to yourself: "I am the observer of this emotion, and I accept it as it is right now."

In this 'witness' state of consciousness, you will come to realize that you exist beyond emotions – and this realization is the true nature of peace itself. It's because you are that peace, that it is possible for you to observe any form of agitation, like fear, sadness or anger.

Whatever happens to the body, the mind or the emotional system, it never happens to your true nature.

OBSERVATION

~~~~~~~~~~~~~~~~~~~~~

Observation allows us
to see reality as a whole
without projecting ourselves into it.

At a seminar, I invited participants to make a drawing that was to represent life. With the exception of one participant, they all did just that – they drew all sorts of things that represented life to them. At the end of the exercise we reviewed the drawings. But reaching the last person, the participants were all surprised to see only a blank sheet.

One person said, "You don't have to participate, but then why are you here?" She didn't understand that this participant had in fact represented the essence of life – as an immense blank white field where all the vast amount of things in the world being just a projection.

If you pause and observe right now for even just a moment, what do you actually see that you would call life? A room perhaps, maybe people, or perhaps the vastness of nature – and at the same time as you experience all your sensory inputs, notice that they are being mixed with your thoughts about everything you see and hear, along with the continual free-association of past and future imaginings, plus your inner accumulation of memories, attitudes, anticipations, concepts, prejudices and assumptions.

All of these experiences, thoughts, memories and imaginations – in neurological reality – are actually happening not in the outside world, but inside our heads. We call all this activity our experience of life, but it's in fact our projections onto life, not life itself. Life is a vast blank canvas upon which our mind tirelessly colors its own sensory inputs, memories, thoughts, projections and imaginations.

What I am suggesting is that we regularly stop and step back from our chronic projections onto life – and instead, be the neutral witness or observer of the process that generates our experience in life. Through this detached awareness, we can perceive neutrality in everything – and we can experience directly the energetic background of life's manifestation. This is a good way to transcend the illusion of duality, to distance ourselves from the body's ongoing reactions, and become grounded in our true identity.

ENSLAVEMENT

~~~~~~~~~~~~~~~~~~

*In order to be truly free
make sure that you never
put your own inner feelings
in the hands of others.*

Imagine that a man tells you he controls your life, and that he requires you to get up every day at three in the morning, eat only beans, dress in a specific way, and do work you don't like. You would probably immediately rebel, proclaiming that you have not submitted to him, and refuse to run your life based on his edicts.

This example deals with external factors, but in your inner life, you'll probably find that feelings of subjugation predominate in your inner space. Specifically, how you feel each moment is being determined by how people around you react or respond to you.

Consider the following: a woman has spent two hours preparing a delicious meal. While her guests eat, one of them tells her that in fact he doesn't like the food he's eating – and her joy of just a few seconds before vanishes immediately. A feeling of discomfort suddenly overwhelms her, causing embarrassment and perhaps even a sense of worthlessness.

Unconsciously, that woman has just subjected her feelings to someone else's judgment. Most of us habitually adopt such behavior, but that's no reason to consider this as a normal healthy situation. If someone has the power to determine your feelings and state of mind, then you are in fact enslaved.

Even if you've spent ten years preparing a professional project which ends up being criticized by your superior, this rejection should never be given the power to throw you off balance. When your relationship with your 'earthly team' becomes strong enough, you will no longer give your power away to others.

Create and nurture a harmonious relationship with your 'earthly team', and no one will ever again have control over your feelings and inner condition.

THE FREE BEING
~~~~~~~~~~~~~~~~~~

A conditioned being
has learned to control life.
A free being has learned
to dance with it.

We all yearn to feel free – but what does it mean to be a free being? Free beings attach no importance to their past or their future. Only the present moment is observed and responded to as reality. Furthermore, free beings don't need the approval of others, because the fear of not being loved has purposefully been let go of.

Also, free beings don't seek to accumulate knowledge and understanding through theories, but rather through life experience. And they don't feel lonely, because they have witnessed directly that nothing and no one is separate. They live their lives without effort or desire, but instead with amusement and curiosity.

Conditioned beings claim to know innumerable things. They're always looking for signs, and they spend a lot of energy in order to understand their past sufferings. Free beings know that they know nothing – so they keep on flowing from one discovery to the next.

There are three pillars of experience that readily open up and support the exploration of new dimensions in the realm of living free:

1) **Detachment**: free beings can fully appreciate every moment, yet without clinging in any way to that moment or experience. They embrace everything that comes into their lives, but let go immediately without resistance.

2) **Perception**: free beings look at what happens around and within them beyond the blinders of duality. They intimately know that every circumstance is an opportunity for blossoming.

3) **Gratitude**: free beings recognize that every present moment is a gift offered by life, and they openly and kindly cherish whatever comes their way.

YOU ARE THE KEY
~~~~~~~~~~~~~~~~~~~~~~~~~~~

*Relief is not found through seeking
the key to end all your worries.
Your quest for relief ends when
you realize that you are the key.*

You have probably put into practice many astute ideas to improve your life and made numerous plans regarding how to become fulfilled. Maybe you've tried to adopt a new way of thinking and perhaps an entirely new approach to life – you have certainly tried various methods and tools, always hoping to discover one change that could finally bring you inner harmony.

Have you been successful? Did you find your magic wand? Undoubtedly not. Over time, the effects of all these attempts at change have inevitably faded, and for only one reason: there is no tool other than yourself that can forever transform your life.

This is not a great revelation, since deep-down you know this truth intimately. So why spend your energy trying to find something you already embody? I have a

136

challenge for you. Whenever you are looking for an external solution, repeat to yourself:

"I don't need a solution, because I AM the solution."

After you begin to hold this statement in the back of your mind, observe what happens in the following minutes, hours or days. Does your life begin to change and improve all on its own, when you're simply being genuine in your dealings with the world?

Remember that it's crucial to avoid having any expectations, since anticipation freezes a situation.

You can repeat this sentence regularly to yourself in a fully conscious manner. Remain detached to outcomes, and you will see that life will soon present you with optimum solutions to your dilemmas.

Without any effort or the exertion of willpower, you will find harmony within yourself and through your life.

HAPPINESS

~~~~~~~~~~~~~~~~~~~~

We can never make ourselves happy
or go out and acquire happiness —
the contented feeling we hunger for
already resides within us.

A rich tourist got lost in a small village some distance from a large city. He went over to one of the locals sitting at an out-door café. "Excuse me, madam," he said, approaching her. "I'm on holiday, trying to find the town center and its beautiful church and museum."

She looked calmly at the man for a moment, then smiled. "You seem to be quite lost," she said, noting that he was looking at the surroundings with a certain disdain. "You know, I was once like you. Chasing after beautiful things, convinced they would make me happy."

"But they do, I enjoy traveling and finding special things to photograph," he insisted. "I have quite a collection now." The lady smiled and said, "I'm sure you do. And those who have ears to hear, can hear what's being said. So I say to you, walk down that street, turn left, walk three blocks, turn right, cross the street and look up – and behold, you have found true happiness."

Confused, the man was silent for a moment. And before leaving, he awkwardly handed the woman a one-dollar bill by way of thanks. The lady politely refused. "You offer me money and it's very nice. And if I could, I would give you my heart so that you may feel this happiness that is already dwelling within you."

Perhaps our primary curse is that we're taught that the external world will bring us all the happiness we hunger for. But even when we surround ourselves with all the things and people we think will make us happy – so often we feel just the opposite, unhappy, depressed, anxious, unwanted and unloved.

It's time to openly agree that nothing can make us happy except our own decision to let ourselves feel happy from the inside-out. We don't need anything at all to be happy. Happiness is rooted within the core of our own being. So let's stop wasting time and energy looking for it elsewhere.

ERROR IS A DECOY
~~~~~~~~~~~~~~~~~~~~~~~

*Learning from our past mistakes
sounds like wise advice –
but in reality it's totally fictitious
because there is no such thing
as a mistake.*

A lot of people think they have made mistakes in their past, and this belief is reinforced by the following sentence I'm sure you already know: "You can learn from your mistakes." And maybe you've followed that advice, hoping to learn more about yourself – and maybe discover from past mistakes, how to avoid new ones.

To all appearances, the suggestion of learning from your past mistakes seems like a wise approach to life. But in reality, it's totally fictitious. Why? For the simple reason that you've never made any errors at all. This may sound very radical, but it has nothing to do with a new belief. In contrast, it stems from existing logic, which I'd like to share with you so that you might stop believing things that aren't in fact logically valid.

It's only possible to assume we made a mistake in the past, if we can compare two situations that are happening simultaneously. For example, let's say that five years ago, you quit your job – and today you think back, and decide that quitting your job was a mistake.

Well, now look around you and ask yourself: "Do I now see the situation in which I should have been, if I haven't chosen to quit my job five years ago?" No, in reality there is no other situation, except the situation you're experiencing right now. As you don't have the possibility to compare two situations which are happening simultaneously in your present moment, you don't have the possibility to say that quitting your job was an error either. The following beliefs like "I have made a mistake" or "I could have done this better" or "this situation should be different than what it is" only exist in an imaginary state, but they have nothing to do with reality.

When we realize this truth, then we won't waste any more precious energy imagining things that don't exist at all outside our imagination. There are no mistakes!

INTUITION
~~~~~~~~~~~~~~~~~~~~~~~

Never take for granted
what you've been told.
Validate everything
through your intuition,
which will guide you
through each new moment.

When we speak about intuition, most of the time we think that it's something related to our feelings. You've probably heard that sentence: "Follow your heart, follow your feelings." But from my understanding, intuition doesn't have anything to do with heart and feelings. Intuition is instead a direct path, and never uses feelings to communicate with us.

Imagine the following situation, which I'm sure you've already experienced: You get a call and without looking at your phone, you suddenly know who is calling you. You didn't ask yourself any questions to know who was calling you, nor didn't you feel any kind of emotion –

you received that information from your intuition, from a neutral state of mind.

So – how do you know if something really resonates as intuitive insight? It's very simple. If the hunch or insight or answer you receive is totally devoid of feelings, then your intuition is speaking to you at that very moment. Intuition leaves you with the impression that "I know what I have to do, but I can't explain how I know it – I just know!"

The very first inner information we receive in a situation always stems from our intuition, which is not logical at all. But because we're trained to ignore our deeper impulses and instead respond automatically to the voice of our conditioning, we tend to trust deductive reasoning and programmed reactions to motivate our actions.

Every human being is from birth endowed with intuition, it's a natural skill. And to tap intuition, just observe the body. If it's tense and focused on the outer world, you've lost connection with the inner world of the intuition. And when the body is relaxed and breathing from the belly, you know you're in tune with your deeper voice, guided by your intuitive wisdom.

~~~~~~~~~~~~~~~~~~~~~~~~~~

YOU ARE YOUR OWN GUIDE

~~~~~~~~~~~~~~~~~~~~~~

Liberty belongs to those
who have the courage to be
their own guide.

A student said to his master:
"I long to be like you."
The master replied calmly:
"In doing so, you would spend your life
trying to be like someone else."
Surprised, the student added:
"But I need an example for guidance."
"Of course," retorted the master,
"but the example is none other than yourself."
"In that case, what is the reason
for my presence here?"
asked the student, confused.
"You are here to remember that truth,"
concluded the teacher, smiling.

One day, I decided to quit my job. But a friend advised
me somewhat anxiously: "You make a good living now.

If I were you, I wouldn't change my job." For all her kindness to me, my friend didn't realize that she was projecting her own fears onto me.

Optimally, others should never project their perspective onto our situation, even if it seems familiar to them, because the way they see the situation undeniably stems from their own highly personal experience. So don't let yourself be swayed overmuch by the opinions and illusory comparisons of others. Always remember the key point: you are your own guide.

The logic is clear: because you are unique, no one but yourself can serve as an example to you. So I invite you to turn your eyes as often as possible away from the outside world's influence. Consciously tune into the body's breathing, as you relax and detach yourself from the opinions of other people.

Focus your attention naturally inward. Be guided by your authentic inner voice of wisdom. It alone knows what really suits you, and following this wisdom will help you shape your life in a unique way. Then you can let your light shine forth in all its splendor!

WAKE UP!
~~~~~~~~~~~~~~~~~~~~~

Why do the same bothersome things
keep repeating, day after day?
Are we stuck forever in
those same old repetitive
patterns and feelings?

Your alarm rings, you open your eyes and at that moment, all your accumulated illusions about who you are get projected onto this new moment and day. Without realizing it, your memory plays the same trick on you every morning, reminding you of your name, your age, your pains, your illnesses, your flaws. You remember the mistakes and sufferings of your past, your deepest fears and failures, and especially your inability to extricate yourself from a web of memories in which you are stuck like a mosquito ready to be eaten.

Why is it that, despite all the work you've done on yourself, nothing really changes? Why are you faced eternally with so many repetitive patterns? Perhaps it's because every morning when you first wake up, you automatically allow your memory to reactivate beliefs and stories that are not real.

You wake up but perhaps you stay asleep – dreaming a particular story of who you are – a story that usually doesn't serve you well at all.

Imagine that you are looking down at the body when you wake up in the morning – look at that body while the conditioning projects all old memories onto the body. Observe this auto-program mechanism in a fully conscious manner, and you will begin to free yourself from its influence.

You have the capacity to truly wake up anew each morning, into a fresh present-moment that allows you to embrace not the past of who you have been, but instead the present – in which you can emerge as a unique new creation.

Tomorrow, if you open your eyes to this world, say to yourself the following sentence: "All these habitual thoughts moving through the mind don't reflect who I really am."

Tomorrow, wake up to the new true you!

HUMANITY
~~~~~~~~~~~~~~~~~~~~~~

Humanity is like a gigantic organ
which contains billions of cells.
This organ can only be healthy
when all the cells are working
harmoniously together.

When we look at humanity as a whole, we naturally hope that it is functioning like a healthy living organ. And it will only be possible for that organ to be healthy, if each and every one of its cells is in good health.

On a biological level, vitality emerges when cellular interconnections are clear and functioning naturally, responding to the needs of every single cell in the body. Illness develops when cells are isolated, not connected to the whole, cut off from their environment. When individual cells don't receive the information and nurturing they need to function properly, they experience cellular stress. This stress creates a rejection reaction that leads to malfunction and then disease, because the body can't handle confusion and stress in the long run.

Human beings are all interconnected at many different levels ranging from visual/vocal communication to tech/media connections, and emotional, resonant and telepathic planes. We can feel what's happening right now all around the world. From this perspective there are no separate "personal problems" – what we're feeling is collective and inherent to what humanity is experiencing at this moment.

I've seen so many people struggling against their particular disease. Unfortunately, fighting against a problem always reinforces it by creating more tension, more stress and more anxiety – not only on a personal level, but also affecting humanity as a whole. When one of us rejects a fear, it goes into the collective consciousness, adding to humanity's fearful feeling.

You're capable of catching both information and emotions from the outer world. Humanity is a great telepathic whole – and the problems we're facing don't necessarily stem from our personal experience. So whatever emotions you experience, please accept them, even if they're not specifically yours. This is how you can offer compassionate help to all of humanity.

GENUINE WISDOM

~~~~~~~~~~~~~~~~~~~~~~~

Wisdom comes from honest
acceptance of what's real and true.
Genuine wisdom realizes that
we have nothing to gain
because we already have
everything we need.

In the early eighteenth century, a solitary Persian yogi living in a small secluded village attracted the curiosity of thousands of people in his country. All those who came to visit the man seemed to return home peaceful and transformed. An inhabitant of a nearby city, amazed at what he had heard about the yogi, began to search for him.

After three weeks, he finally found his town, and was invited to sit in a small room, where he waited for hours. Having almost lost hope, he finally saw the yogi in the doorway. "Dear yogi, I am honored to meet you," he said, bowing to him. The yogi smiled without saying a word. "I come to see you because I want to find peace in my soul."

The yogi replied, "Very well. From now on, I'll feed you here and offer you everything you need, but on one condition." "What is this condition?" asked the seeker." "You are to sit in this room until you find peace," explained the yogi.

The man did so and after seven days of sitting around doing nothing, he told the yogi: "I still do not feel peace. What am I doing wrong?" The yogi said to him: "Look to see what prevents you from being at peace."

The man resigned himself and tried again. After a month of unremitting efforts to discover what prevented him from finding peace, he came out of the room quite disappointed and told the yogi: "I cannot figure out what prevents me from being at peace."

The wise man looked at him with compassion and said, laughing: "Eureka!"

Wisdom is born of deep insight and returns us to the inescapable evidence that any quest for truth and fulfillment is futile, because everything we seek is already present within us.

SHARING

~~~~~~~~~~~~~~~~~~~

We all aspire toward
abundance in our lives —
but are we ready to share
what we already have?

"What are your wishes of happiness for the world?" asked the teacher to his students. One pupil replied: "I wish for global sharing and world peace." Another one added: "I wish for the protection of animals and nature."

Then a third one said bluntly: "I wish for the extinction of the human species! Only then there will be peace and protection of all living beings on this planet."

Stunned by this upsetting idea, the teacher spoke to him: "Don't you think that human beings can improve?" The child stared at him and replied: "I live alone with my disabled mother. Lately we hardly have enough money to eat — will you help us?"

Embarrassed, the professor remained silent, for he had no genuine impulse to share his abundance.

It's so often true – there exists a very real gap between what humans desire for the world, and what they are personally prepared to offer. And as long as they consider themselves to be distinct separate individuals in the world, nothing of importance will change to improve humanity as a whole.

As soon as every human being understands that humanity is its family and that global well-being inevitably influences personal well-being, then the world's condition will improve.

Once we accept our interdependence with all living things on this planet, and no longer fixate only on our individual well-being, then we can offer our help spontaneously, and even for no apparent reason. We no longer feel the need to demand anything in return, because we understand that our helpful deeds and contributions will prove also ultimately beneficial to ourselves.

Everything we offer to others is a gift to ourselves. So what are we willing to offer today, right now, to those in need?

KNOWLEDGE
~~~~~~~~~~~~~~~~~

*You can go and learn
about countless things
but they will never reveal
your own true nature.*

A teacher on vacation went searching to discover facts about the historical heritage of an old Iranian citadel. He stopped in front of an imposing statue on which was written: "Only life lives on, because time erases everything else in its path."

Intrigued, the teacher wrote down this sentence in his little notebook. Behind another vestige, he saw an old yogi sitting without moving, dressed in a dusty cloth. Discreetly and without wanting to bother him, the teacher started to walk away, then suddenly heard: "What are you looking for here?"

The teacher jumped and turned around. "I'm a history teacher and I'm looking for a new interesting topic for my students," he said. "A history topic? Don't you find such things to be an absolute futility?" asked the yogi.

154

The historian felt offended and replied, "Well, remaining seated there meditating certainly won't lead to any new knowledge." The yogi calmly responded: "Human beings explore the depths of the ocean and the vastness of the universe, but what do they know about their own selves? The most interesting subject is none other than oneself, because everything else fades with time."

Many facts and accounts have accumulated concerning your personality, which you've integrated into your idea of who you are. But what do you know about yourself apart from all that has been said about you? Is this acquired knowledge really shedding light on your true nature and purpose? I invite you to question everything you think you know about yourself, and indeed, about life as a whole.

When you start looking at who you are beyond all your historic facts and stories, you become free to explore more honestly your own inner nature. If you wish to make new discoveries, it's always first necessary to shed all forms of prior knowledge – only then can you take the plunge and dive eagerly into the world of the unknown.

THE HUMAN BEING
~~~~~~~~~~~~~~~~~~~~~

What is the difference between
an animal and a human being?
Animals adjust to nature —
but humans require that
nature adjust to them.

A participant said to me:
"The world is in a growing chaos.
This must be remedied."

And I responded:

What needs to be done ... will be done.

"You speak to me as if the imbalance
will disappear on its own."

Life maintains its balance at every moment.

"At this moment, countless humans die."

At this moment, countless cells die in your body.
Life is just like this body.
Everything naturally regulates itself.

"How dare you compare humans to a single cell?"

Why do you see differences where there are none?
Life flows in everything with the same intensity.

"Humanity is in crisis!"

The crisis is within you.
Humanity is the extension of you.

"Are my prayers in vain?"

Do you think that by setting out good intentions
the world will change?
Stop looking outward for a moment and
observe what is happening within you.

"You ask me to do nothing to help the world?"

If you can first be at peace, then life will do the rest.

"Humanity holds an important place on Earth!"

Yes, it is just as important as the rest.
That's what we overlook most of the time…

THE DIVINE
~~~~~~~~~~~~~~~~~~~

The divine is not within you –
it is you.
So stop looking for it.
Just be aware of it
and your own light
will illumine the way for you.

One day, a young man went in search of God. He traveled constantly across great spaces, looking everywhere – but in all his efforts, he did not find God. Resigned to failure, he decided to go back home.

On the way home, he crossed paths with a wise old man. Feeling the need for comfort, the young man stopped and looked into the deep blue eyes of the elder. "Old wise man," he asked politely, "would you do me the honor of a conversation?"

With a nod, he was invited to sit down. Looking hesitant, he explained: "I was told that God exists, and I was assured that God's voice could be heard. I've addressed all my questions to God's presence, but have received no response. All my efforts have been in vain."

The sage stared at the upset young man and replied: "My boy, I'm sorry to disappoint you. But God can neither be heard nor seen."

The young man felt somewhat annoyed. "But we've heard so much about God – is there really no way of knowing that God really exists."

The old man smiled: "Simply look – you are the living proof that God exists."

You cannot observe even your own true nature. Since you're never separated from it, it's impossible for you to describe it, to feel it or give it a name. So, stop searching. Just be aware of your own divine presence.

Your essence cannot be contained in words or concepts because your essence is the container. When you realize that you are the only reality and that you contain absolutely everything, then nothing besides pure essence will have any influence on you.

DEATH

~~~~~~~~~~~~~~~~~~~~

*Our linear-time mortal life
and our thoughts and
memories do definitely die.
However, who we really are
transcends space and time.*

I was accompanying a terminally ill person who told me, with a heavy heart, "Today I'm celebrating my eighty-sixth anniversary. I am close to death and I'm so afraid of it. I'll have to give up everything I've built in my life, even if I don't want to. All that energy invested in fulfilling my dreams – in the end, I leave empty handed."

"In life, nothing is permanent – the body and thoughts are continually changing. We possess certain things, then we lose them again. This is part of the ongoing movement of life. But your essence was never born, so it can't die" I answered.

What are we beyond the body, thoughts and emotions? We know at our core that there's an eternal nonphysical realm of life that we're all welcome to live within. Let's stop attaching too much importance to our success, our possessions, all the concepts and stories we've learned, how we think and react and so forth – because yes, all this will vanish at the end of this human life.

On the other hand, our essence cannot be quantified or altered or destroyed by time. If we approach life with the acceptant awareness that nothing is ever permanent, we become happily detached from clinging to everything around us. We come to understand that it's useless to hold on to anything, because everything disappears sooner or later.

I'm inviting you to observe a natural mechanism that is specific to life: by accepting this reality that the physical, mental and emotional presence we so often identify with will surely disappear in the natural course of things, we can live more intensely and in peace.

In other words, ultimately we have nothing to lose and nothing to gain. What we truly are is and always will be. So with all things considered, what is there to chase after in the end?

LOOSING SOMEONE
~~~~~~~~~~~~~~~~~~~~~

*You can't lose anyone
because separation
doesn't exist.*

A widowed man came to a consultation and told me: "I lost my wife, while she was giving birth to our son. And one year ago, my son died in a car accident. I tried to commit suicide, but unfortunately I'm still alive."

"I'm so sorry to hear that, but why did you try to commit suicide?" I asked gently.

"Because I wanted to be again with my wife and my son," he answered, crying.

"And what if, even after death, you couldn't go back to them?" I continued.

He looked at me surprised and replied: "At least I would have tried."

"It may sound radical," I said to him honestly, "but you'll never again see your loved ones."

"Why are you so harsh with me when I'm suffering?"

"You are suffering because you believe you're separated from loved ones who have died. But hear me, please – you can never lose your loved ones, there can never be any separation between you and them. Your death won't change anything. The love you feel for your wife and son is alive right now and always within you. Love brings all illusory separation into a unique inner center. Love cannot be lost - it is omnipresent and lives within you. It's the illusion of separation that makes you suffer. So you can relax, and open up to feel the presence of your loved ones with you, right now. "

He took a deep breath, seemed to shift his entire posture, wiped his eyes of tears, and softly said to me: "I can't understand everything that you're telling me, but deep in my heart, I hear you – and strangely, I'm suddenly feeling wonderfully full in my heart. I haven't felt this lightness for years. What's happening?"

"You just abandoned yourself to your own life energy and to the wisdom of eternal love. And as you can feel, deep inside yourself, peace always remains."

SPIRITUALITY
~~~~~~~~~~~~~~~~~

We hope that spiritual guides
will somehow come to us and
show us what to do with our life —
but in truth it is always our
own infinite presence
who speaks to us.

"I've been told that there are spiritual guides, beings of light and intuition who will come and guide me," a participant inquired. "But how do I access these guides — and who am I in all this?"

One person teaches us one thing, and another teaches us something different — and we find ourselves no closer to the truth. The truth is in fact obvious, it's not a shifting malleable belief. Truth is permanent, not subject to any change, and comes to us spontaneously, unveiled and revealed — but only when we finally cease identifying with what we are not.

We believe that spiritual guides and intuitive realizations exist out there somewhere. Such experiences are possible only because and above all, we ourselves exist. If we no longer exist, then the guide, the intuition, life itself no longer has grounds to be.

When you talk to your guide and it answers you, who is actually talking at that moment? When you receive information from your intuition, where does that information come from? Do you believe that there exists anything else besides you in your experiential world? Isn't the outside world, including your spiritual guides and intuition, in fact your own reflection – is there anything entirely separate from your inner awareness?

You as a conscious living presence existed prior to any manifestation, and for any manifestation to appear, you must first be. So focus on realizing the truth – who is the guide who speaks to you, if not yourself?

Instead of seeking imaginary guides who will speak to you, the wise path is to let all the spiritual games go, and see your essence in everything.

THE PURPOSE OF LIFE
~~~~~~~~~~~~~~~~~~~~~~~~~~~

Only those who reject their past-sufferings
are in search of their purpose in life.
Those who have totally accepted their past
don't search anything.
They live in constant bliss.

"What is my mission in life?" a young man asked me urgently – to which I replied: "Every quest is driven by a concept. If you are searching for your life mission, it is because you are blinded by illusory imperfections about yourself. In reality, you have no task to accomplish, no mission – because everything happens naturally in its own good time."

"So what am I useful for?" he asked, and I answered: "Life is sufficient unto itself. So you can stop searching – any such attempt is futile. Instead of chasing after concepts, summon the courage to observe and participate in what is spontaneously happening. As your quest vanishes, you'll discover the splendor of your essence being reborn in every instant."

When we live intensely every moment in a state of communion with All That Is, we have no need to attach importance to finding our purpose in life. But when we become lost in our thoughts, engulfed in questions about meaning and purpose, we miss experiencing the very essence of life.

We employ reasoning in order to grab hold of life – even though upon honest observation, we can see that the ever-emerging newness of life itself can't be manipulated by intellectual gymnastics.

Most people consider questions like "Why was I born?" or "What is my mission in life?" or "What is the purpose of life?" to be highly spiritual inquiries. Yet these questions all reflect a profound misunderstanding of the essence of life. In reality there can be no purpose to life, because life doesn't aspire to anything – life in itself is perfect, right here and right now.

These questions of purpose never arise when the inherent greatness of life is directly perceived and embraced. When we realize that there's nothing that's in need of our improvement, the notion of purpose disappears. The word "why" drops away, ushering in a natural state of continual acceptance and bliss.

YOU ARE NOT RESPONSIBLE

~~~~~~~~~~~~~~~~~~~~~~

*Since you're not responsible
for the creation of your body,
you can't be responsible
for the life that stems from it.*

During one of my seminars, a participant shared with me: "A spiritual teacher told me that I was responsible for my life. Maybe he wouldn't have told me this, if he knew what I had been through." "Would you like to share with us your story?" I asked him. He took all his courage and whispered:

"A few years ago, I accidentally ran over my two year old son. Since the spiritual teacher told me that I was responsible for my life, which means that I'm also responsible for my son's life, I can't sleep and eat anymore. I feel so guilty that I just want to die."

We've often heard that we are responsible for our lives. But before assuming this, we have to question ourselves on a deeper level. Life starts with a body. It's the body that makes life possible - without a body, we couldn't experience this earthly dimension. So the first question is: "Are we responsible for the creation of this body, or did the body develop itself naturally?"

We have to recognize that this physical miracle did everything on its own, and without our help. In fact, it possesses its own wisdom and intelligence. Since we are not responsible for the creation of that body, we can't be responsible for that life, which stems from that body.

There are millions of people who are suffering from that illusory responsibility which makes them feel guilty, sometimes even to the point where they believe the only way to free themselves from that heavy weight is to commit suicide.

When we consciously look at life, without any conditioned barrier or programming, then we can realize that life itself has never asked us to feel responsible or guilty about what the body has done.

From this viewpoint, you are now free to give yourself the chance to start a new life, by choosing to put aside all judgmental concepts and assumptions your mind's conditioning created, which have nothing to do with life itself.

PART SEVEN

The Witness

~~~~~~~~~~~~~~~~~~~~

"You are witnessing life,
but you never were alive."

OBSERVING THE MOVIE

*Life can be seen
as a film that you
are currently watching
with total absorption.*

Imagine you are in a movie theater with a large white screen onto which a flood of sights and sounds are being projected. The movie is called 'The Life of a Human Being'. You are so taken in by the drama and stimulation of the film that you temporarily forget that you're simply a member of the audience.

You unconsciously identify quite completely with the main character and get caught up in the impression of living her or his life – and even feeling her or his emotions. You weep and laugh with the character, love and hate, struggle and triumph as the plot unfolds.

While the film plays, you become completely absorbed by the images shown on the screen. You temporarily forget that in reality, beyond the confines of the theater production, you're a member of the audience, you're not involved on the screen at all.

This example is not fictitious – every day you and all the people around you wake up to the dominating sounds and images of your intense dramatic life-plot on this shared world stage. You wake up and reflexively merge your identity with the physical human being who's starring in your movie. You temporarily lose sight of the essential behind your movie identity: the silent observer exists beyond the drama of the film.

What do you think will happen to you when this film, this life you're witnessing, will end? From the point of view of the audience, of the witness – absolutely nothing. From this perspective, the vagaries of mortal human life have zero power to influence you.

Do you think you have been born and are doomed to die? Not from the perspective of the witness who lives outside the movie, who continues beyond this world's perceptual illusion of drama-infused dualism.

Isn't it wonderful to step back and calmly observe that life unfolds spontaneously like in a movie, without our needing to intervene – and that ultimately beyond all the drama, nothing can ever affect us?

THE ILLUSORY PRESENT MOMENT
~~~~~~~~~~~~~~~~~~~~~~~~~~~

When you're aware that your true nature
is prior to space and time,
then you don't try to anchor yourself
into the present moment,
because you suddenly realize that
the present moment doesn't exist.

We were taught that only the present moment exists; perhaps we did a lot of exercises to anchor ourselves in it. Meditation is one of the tools that was designed to help us be aware of the present moment. A lot of spiritual approaches explain that living consciously in the present moment can lead us to our fulfillment.

But is the present moment the only reality we are living in? What if the present moment is a springboard into another dimension? Let's reconsider the assumption that the present moment is the 'final destination', Reflect on the following questions and answers:

Who is reading this text right now? (The mind, which is intimately bound to the body.)

Are you that mind which is reading this question? (To be aware of an existing mind, we already must be outside of the mind. This means that we are the observer of the mind and not the mind itself. And if we aren't the mind itself, we can't be the body nor the emotional system which are bound to the mind.)

So who is actually reading this text? (Only a human being with whom we identify very often, who is always living in the present moment because it can't escape from it – that's why meditation isn't needed for the human being to anchor itself in the present moment.)

The deeper truth is that we're observing not only the human being reading this text, we're also observing the present moment itself! And to be doing this, to be witnessing the body and the present moment, we must be existing in a dimension that exists totally beyond space and time.

Our true nature isn't bound to the physical reality in which this human being is in this present moment reading this text. Our true nature is the source of time and space and all that's arising in it – the manifest world. The body lives in the present moment, but our true nature transcends three-dimensional reality.

YOU CAN'T SUFFER
~~~~~~~~~~~~~~~~~~~~~

Only illusion induces suffering.
Reality is painless.

A participant asked me:

"I've done several therapies searching for mental and emotional health, looking for the causes of my illness, but without any success. If only I could find the moment when all this suffering started…"

And I responded:

The suffering starts now.

"But yesterday I felt very bad already."

This is what you imagine now. There is nothing else than the present moment here. Suffering takes place only in the now. And therefore it's only in the now that the suffering could disappear, if you would allow it.

"But I really want this illness to disappear!"

Then be free of any intention. When you let go of the intention to be healed, the suffering will disappear. You are not that being who is suffering. You're only its witness. Your true nature can't suffer. Like a reflection in the mirror, the suffering appears to be real to you. But you're neither the mirror, nor its reflection. Only illusion induces suffering. Reality is painless.

"All the therapists I've met have told me the importance of working on my inner suffering…"

Why make so much fruitless labor? Suffering is only the result of dead memories projected onto the present moment. No work can liberate you of the illusion of being something that you're not.

"So – suffering doesn't exist?"

If you look at life assuming that you are what is happening inside the body, then surely it will induce suffering. However, when you look at life through the eyes of your true nature, then you'll see the world for what it really is.

"What is that world you're talking about?"

It is the clear reflection of your perfection.

LIFE ORCHESTRATES EVERYTHING
~~~~~~~~~~~~~~~~~~~~~~~~~~~~~

The heart is beating without our intervention.
The body is managing itself spontaneously.

Life moves the body in various directions
without our help.

Thoughts and emotions appear
and dissolve naturally.

Intuition occurs suddenly
without any anticipation.

So how can you pretend
to be running your life?

A participant asked me: "Many spiritual approaches say that we are in charge of life, that we have to control it in a certain way so that we can manifest what we really want. Is this true?" I asked in return: "Can you control all the functions of your body right now?" This was his answer: "No. I can only help the body on a certain level." And I continued: "Isn't it the body that's taking care for itself at every single moment?" And he said: "Well, I give my body food and water so that it can survive." To which I replied: "Doesn't the body nourish itself? If it is hungry now, it stands up and it goes looking for some food. Then it swallows the food and digests it. Isn't the body, and only the body, doing all this?"

After a moment, he said, "I never looked at the body from that point of view – it's disconcerting." And I said: "Life is a self-motivating energy that manages itself beautifully in every new moment. We're unable to manage all the millions of functions taking place inside the body, so how could we possibly manage the vastness of life?" He replied: "But I've been told many times that I have the ability and responsibility to take charge and manage my life."

And I responded: "There is no such thing as 'my' life. There prevails only life. And when you stop identifying with this human shape, you attain an extraordinary and global vision of life itself. The idea of creating something stems from the belief that there is something missing, or that life as it actually is, must be changed. If you look at life through the eyes of your true nature, you'll realize that life is already perfect."

THE PARADOX

~~~~~~~~~~~~~~~~~~~~

Unification isn't possible
because now and always
there is no separation at all.

A participant told me: "I was at a seminar where we were invited to reconnect ourselves with our divine part. During meditation I felt a powerful energy flowing through my body. Was this my divine part?"

I answered: "While doing this exercise, you believed it was possible to be in contact with your divine part. This creates the idea that you have to do something to get in touch with your divine part. This idea maintains the illusion of separation. You've heard that your true nature is somewhere out there, out of reach. There are so many theories – but the truth isn't a concept. If just for an instant you forget all you've heard about having a divine part, you will immediately realize that it's impossible to get in touch with your divine part."

"I'm very confused right now," replied the participant, shaking his head in dismay.

I smiled. "Good. Confusion is wonderful, because from it emerges inner clarity. Observe for instance that you can't ever get in touch and feel your true nature's energy, because you already fully embody it."

In actual fact, we'll never experience a reunion with our true nature, because there is no separation between us and our divine part. We can observe and feel only that which isn't us. So let's stop looking for something that we already are – we are already fully divine.

There are many theories which invite us to do something in order to reach and merge with our so-called higher self. However, the false belief that there exists a separate part of us only reinforces the idea of a fictitious separation from our true nature. This is the main reason for all our so called spiritual quests.

We've been trained to think that we're a soul experiencing itself through a body, and after death our soul will then explore other dimensions and hopefully return to its true self. This whole belief system is based on the notion of separation, even when we assume that there prevails only Oneness. This paradox will disappear as soon as we stop searching for what we already and eternally are.

THE WITNESS

~~~~~~~~~~~~~~~~~~~~

You are witnessing life,
but you are not alive.

I invite you to do a little exercise. Simply stay in front of a mirror and look at the body – and observe how suddenly the idea of you being that body arises. We assume that the belief "I am my body" always existed, but if we look at a very young child, this perception doesn't exist at all, early in life. This identification was created through repetition. When that young child fell down, people said: "Did you hurt *yourself?*"

Finally, by hearing the word "yourself" thousands of times, this belief took root, and started to expand to also include the mind and the emotions. And thus in your developing self-concept, you not only became a body, but also thoughts and emotions.

Now look again to that mirror and ask yourself: "Am I that body – or am I the observer of that body?" The truth is, you are only that body's witness.

Now ask yourself: "Am I the thought 'I'm not that body' or am I the observer of that thought?" Again you can see that you're witnessing that thought. Apply the same observation for an emotion. When you say "I'm sad," you are not actually that sadness – you're the neutral observer of that emotion. And everything that you can observe cannot be you.

During all these years, you've believed you are a physical being with problems, emotional suffering, getting ill and feeling alone, needing to accomplish something in life – and also that you finally must die.

Now you realize that you didn't do any of these experiences – only the human being did. You have no mission on earth, because your true nature has never entered that dimension.

I encourage you as the life witness to lovingly nurture that human being that you're not, by regularly affirming: "Dear human being, whether you are rich or poor, in good health or not, attaining your dreams or failing them, it doesn't matter at all – I love you just as you are right now."

THE DREAM OF YOUR LIFE
~~~~~~~~~~~~~~~~~~~~~~~~~

Life is like a dream
in which you imagine
being someone.

A participant asked me:

"When certain situations recur, my feelings of joy
dissipate suddenly and my old reactions reappear.
I then feel overwhelmed by fear."

And I responded:

Observe that fear, without interfering with it. Look at it as if
you were looking at a cloud. Don't try to transform or dissipate
it – and you'll see that fear is really like a cloud.
It appears and suddenly disappears.
You can't catch fear, because it doesn't exist in reality.

"But then why am I so afraid of death?"

Because you believe that you were born.

"But we both seem very alive now!"

You only see your projections.
You perceive a fictitious person who you call Nassrine
and you automatically think that this person is me.

But this person has no common points with my true nature.
How could I die, if I was never born? And what is a person?
Fundamentally it is an assembly of memories.
You were told that you were born at a particular moment.
But except what others told you about that birth,
did you ever experience birth? Can you actually remember it?
Can you specifically detect the moment when you
suddenly thought that you were alive?
The idea of being a human came out of the blue.
That belief just suddenly appeared.

"I'm so confused right now."

Only the human being is confused. Don't care about it.

"But ultimately, what is life?"

It is a dream in which you imagine being a person.

"And how can I get out of that dream?"

You can't escape from it for the simple reason
that your true nature never entered that dream.

AWAKENING DOESN'T EXIST
~~~~~~~~~~~~~~~~~~~~~~~~~~

*Where is awakening when the illusion
of being a person disappears?*

A participant asked me:

"I did so many seminars in order to attain awakening,
but I still don't know how to achieve it.

And I responded:

Well, you actually can't.

"I've heard stories about people who achieved it."

As you say, they're only stories.

"But there are a lot of spiritual teachers
teaching us different tools to attain awakening."

*To say "I'm awakened" you first have to be a person.
But in reality that "me" doesn't exist.
It's just a feeling of being, and all feelings are illusory.*

186

Those who pretend to be enlightened are confusing themselves
with a person. But where is awakening, if the illusion
of being a person disappears?

"This is so different from what I've heard.
It's obvious, but it's confusing my mind."

You don't have to care about the mind,
because your true nature doesn't own one.
Your true nature can't claim to be something in particular.
It has no intentions, it can't experience anything.
It simply is.

"So then, all my quests were in vain?"

There never was a quest.
All that searching only happened
through the illusion of being someone.
There is only what is,
And what is, can't be explained, nor attained
through any sort of illusory enlightenment.

"But then, what am I?"

Everything except what you think you are.

Final Words

I DON'T WISH YOU ANYTHING

~~~~~~~~~~~~~~~~~~~~~~~~~~~~

So – you had some wishes…

but now you realize that every wish, as noble as it may be,
stems from the non-acceptance of what is here now.

You were willing yourself to be free…

but now you observe that this willpower
maintains the illusion of imprisonment.

You've wanted to integrate new things…

but now you know that the wish to integrate
even the most beautiful thing,
reinforces the idea that you lack something.

You've wanted to be hopeful…

but now you come to the evidence that hope
makes you believe that the current situation isn't perfect.

You had the intention to help others…

but now you realize that having that intention
makes others believe that they're
not sufficient to themselves.

You've wanted to embody love,
wisdom and compassion…

but now you understand that these are mere concepts.

So … I don't wish you anything.

Why?

Because your true nature already contains everything.
Because your true nature is already perfect now.
And because perfection doesn't aspire to anything.

With my luminous thoughts,

Nassrine

~~~~~~~~~~~~~~~~~

Table of Contents

DEDICATION

~~~~~~~~~~~~~~~~~~~~~~~

This wonderful journey has been possible
thanks to the precious presence
of my dearest friends
Mike, Malou and James Anson,
John and Birgitta Selby,
Lili Fournier and Jean Hudon.

www.nassrinereza.com

Printed in Great Britain
by Amazon

58251258R00119